Wordsworth

Wordsworth

Paul Hamilton
Fellow of Exeter College
Oxford

HUMANITIES PRESS INTERNATIONAL, INC.
Atlantic Highlands, NJ

First published in 1986 in the United States of America by
HUMANITIES PRESS INTERNATIONAL, INC.,
Atlantic Highlands, NJ 07716

© Paul Hamilton, 1986

Library of Congress Cataloging-in-Publication Data

Hamilton, Paul, D. Phil.
　Wordsworth—a critical introduction.

　(Harvester new readings)
　Bibliography: p.
　1. Wordsworth, William, 1770–1850—Criticism and
interpretation.　I. Title.　II. Series.
PR5888.H36　1986　　821′.7　　86-326
ISBN 0-391-03417-0

PRINTED IN GREAT BRITAIN

I am very grateful to Kelvin Everest, who persuaded me to write this book, and who supplied encouraging and constructively critical responses to various drafts, as did Marilyn Butler and Heather Glen. My thanks to them, and to the two anonymous Harvester readers from whose forceful reactions I learnt much in contradictory ways. Most of my ideas have been tried out on patient or protesting students at Oxford and elsewhere, and to them I am indebted for the ones that work. My daughter Rachel was a model of inarticulacy throughout, and to her the book is dedicated.

Harvester New Readings

This major new series offers a range of important new critical introductions to English writers, responsive to new bearings which have recently emerged in literary analysis. Its aim is to make more widely current and available the perspectives of contemporary literary theory, by applying these to a selection of the most widely read and studied English authors.

The range of issues covered varies with each author under survey. The series as a whole resists the adoption of general theoretical principles, in favour of the candid and original application of the critical and theoretical models found most appropriate to the survey of each individual author. The series resists the representation of any single either traditionally or radically dominant discourse, working rather with the complex of issues which emerge from a close and widely informed reading of the author in question in his or her social, political and historical context.

The perspectives offered by these lucid and accessible introductory books should be invaluable to students seeking an understanding of the full range and complexity of the concerns of key canonical writers. The major concerns of each author are critically examined and sympathetically and lucidly reassessed, providing indispensable handbooks to the work of major English authors seen from new perspectives.

David Aers	*Chaucer*
Drummond Bone	*Byron*
Angus Calder	*T. S. Eliot*
Simon Dentith	*George Eliot*
Kelvin Everest	*Keats*
Kate Flint	*Dickens*
Paul Hamilton	*Wordsworth*
Brean Hammond	*Pope*
Kiernan Ryan	*Shakespeare*
Simon Shepherd	*Spenser*
Nigel Wood	*Swift*

Contents

Note on Editions Used

There is as yet no complete chronological edition of Wordsworth's poetry giving the substantial variants and independent versions of his major works. Jonathan Wordsworth is currently preparing such an edition for Cambridge University Press. The Penguin edition (ed. John O. Hayden; Harmondsworth, 1977), gives much valuable textual and biographical information in its notes, although the poems only appear in their final versions. I have preferred, whenever possible, to use Stephen Gill's easily available selection for *The Oxford Authors* (Oxford, 1984), believing him right to break with most earlier editors by asserting 'that one *must* print a text which comes as close as possible to the state of a poem when it was first completed'. Gill, who is writing a new biography of Wordsworth, also provides useful notes.

For more detailed information on each poem's production, the reader should turn to several excellent editions. I have quoted from *Lyrical Ballads-The Text of the 1798 Edition with the Additional 1800 Poems and the Prefaces*, ed. R. C. Brett and A. R. Jones (London, 1963), and *The Prelude 1799, 1805, 1850*, ed. J. Wordsworth, M. H. Abrams and S. Gill (New York and London, 1979). References to the 1799 *Prelude* are in Roman numerals (e.g. II 159) to distinguish them from references to the 1805 version (e.g. 2.159). For Chapter Two I have used the relevant volumes in *The Cornell Wordsworth*, a meticulously detailed edition being prepared for the professional Wordsworth scholar, but often the only reliable published source for definitive versions of the major poems of the 1790s: *Descriptive Sketches*, ed. Eric Birdsall and P. N. Zall (Ithaca and London, 1984); *An Evening Walk*, ed. James Averill (Ithaca and London, 1984); *The Salisbury Plain Poems*, ed. Stephen Gill (Ithaca and London 1975); *The Ruined Cottage and The Pedlar*, ed. James Butler (Ithaca and London, 1979); *The Borderers* ed. Robert Osborn (Ithaca and London, 1982). In Chapter Four I have quoted from *Home at Grasmere*, ed. Beth Darlington (Ithaca and London, 1977). For Chapter Six I have used *Poems in Two Volumes*, ed. Jared Curtis (Ithaca and London, 1983). The remaining Cornell volumes so far published are *The Prelude, 1798–99*, ed. Stephen Parrish (Ithaca and London, 1977), *Benjamin the Waggoner*, ed. Paul F. Betz (Ithaca and London, 1981) and *The Fourteen-Book 'Prelude'*, ed. W. J. B. Owen (Ithaca and London, 1985). The Introductions to those editions are valuable critical and biographical documents.

Prose quotations come from *The Prose Works of William Wordsworth*, ed. W. J. B. Owen and Jane Smyser (Oxford, 1974). Owen's collection, *Wordsworth's Literary Criticism*, (London, 1974), is usually comprehensive enough. Other essential sources are *Letters of William and Dorothy Wordsworth*, ed. E. de Selincourt, revd Chester L. Shaver and others (Oxford, 1967–); *Journals of Dorothy Wordsworth* ed. Mary Moorman (London, 1971).

Introduction

This book offers a brief, eclectic introduction to some of Wordsworth's major poetry. After a chapter describing a recurrent form of Wordsworthian self-consciousness, the order is chronological up to and including *The Excursion*. Inevitably, in so short a volume, many famous poems are not discussed; but it is hoped that the general argument, at the risk of appearing monotonously consistent, provides a framework for understanding them. The main aim is to give a history of Wordsworth's idea of poetry as it is developed in his poetic writings.

Wordsworth was born in 1770, in the middle of an age whose material and intellectual tendencies led to the French Revolution in 1789. He died in 1850, a Victorian poet-laureate, Browning's 'lost leader' who sold his poetic freedom 'Just for a riband to stick in his coat', a byword for conservatism and an innocuous nature-mysticism. Wordsworth, as Matthew Arnold argued when he rebuked 'the exhibitors and extollers of a "scientific system of thought" in Wordsworth's poetry', frequently has to be rescued from his

1

admirers, and then rescued from admiring rescuers; and this book only adds to their number. After the publication of the long autobiographical poem, The Prelude in 1850, Wordsworth's canon no longer appeared split between the apparent simplicity of Lyrical Ballads of 1798 and 1800, and the increasingly philosophical writings culminating in The Excursion of 1814. Nowadays, with the benefit of the new editions of major works written in the 1790s, and unpublished at the time, we can grasp the range of poetic review of experience which Wordsworth undertook from the start of his poetic career: its ambitiousness matches Milton's justification of God's ways to man, or, nearer in time, Kant's philosophical critique of all inherited modes of thought.

At first there appears to be little connection between the young radical enthusiast, the autobiographical subject of The Prelude, and the man who later accepted a government sinecure. Long before the laureateship he became, in 1813, the Distributor of Stamps for Westmorland, a kind of tax collector who pocketed a percentage of his takings. Reminders of Wordsworth's perennial impecuniousness, or platitudes about how as we grow older we become less radical will not entirely explain the transformation. Nor does William Hazlitt's violent attack on the political views which any government work at that time would imply:

> with one stroke of his prose-pen he disenfranchises the whole rustic population of Westmorland and Cumberland from voting in elections, and says that there is not a man who is not a knave in grain. In return, he lets them still retain the privilege of expressing their sentiments in select and natural language in the Lyrical Ballads.

There is a change of heart standing in need of explanation. When the Whig historian Macaulay read The Prelude, his verdict was unequivocal: 'The poem is to the last degree

Jacobinical, indeed Socialist. I understand perfectly why Wordsworth did not choose to publish it in his lifetime.' Yet the very importance attributed in *The Prelude* to poetry, as the most original and profound mode of understanding, shows political caution. Conversely, as Wordsworth's best critic, Hazlitt, saw, readers scornful of Wordsworth's political timidity should reflect with embarrassment on the poetic gains which were often the result. Unlike Blake, Wordsworth was happy to exploit the fact that polite sympathy with something so impolite as a revolution always implies a studied reserve.

Wordsworth expands poetry's sympathies, and stakes its claims to cultural centrality, in response to the contemporary questioning of institutions of all kinds, fostered by the Enlightenment and culminating in the French Revolution. His work shows the *literary* shape of a liberal's reaction to the new revolutionary possibilities opened up by recent intellectual and political history. He explores in imaginative writing a human potential often existing in opposition to the low esteem in which characters are held by society. Yet in this way he also defends existing forms of social organisation against revolutionary disruptions by making alternative, richer conceptions of people's worth a matter of poetic rather than political endeavour. The poet's metrical art, according to the Preface to *Lyrical Ballads*, is one which pays 'homage...to the elementary principle of pleasure, by which [man] knows, and feels, and lives, and moves', but it is also an art calculated to ensure the immediate excitement thus foregrounded is not 'carried beyond its proper bounds'. Otherwise we would be at the mercy of 'the power of the human imagination' which, the Preface claims, 'is sufficient to produce such changes even in our physical nature as might almost appear miraculous.'

Poetry's increased cultural importance comes from Wordsworth's use of it to accommodate the disturbing new radical sympathies within recollective or traditionally contemplative forms such as tragedy, whose insights are into a formative past or into a condition of human suffering too deep and permanent to be changed by any action. As Walter Pater claimed, Wordsworth taught 'the supreme importance of contemplation in the conduct of life. Contemplation—impassioned contemplation—that is with Wordsworth the end-in-itself, the perfect end.' His political conservatism takes the form of poetic radicalism, lending to poetry a significance rare in its history. We tend, now, to accept unquestioningly the marginal status which poetry occupies amongst other forms of writing in our society. It takes an effort to realise that the choice of poetic expression is an integral part of Wordsworth's liberal philosophy.

Wordsworth's deepest criticism of his society may have been through poetic sympathy, with all the wise passivity that implies, but critique it was, none the less. The fundamental ideal of *The Prelude* is to review contemporary institutions in the light of a poetic re-evaluation of the self for which they legislate—a re-evaluation which at first finds itself in tune with the French Revolution and is given great encouragement by this political corroboration.

> Enough, no doubt, the advocates themselves
> Of ancient institutions had performed
> To bring disgrace upon their very names;
> Disgrace of which custom, and written law,
> And sundry moral sentiments, as props
> And emanations of these institutes,
> Too justly bore a part. A veil had been
> Uplifted. Why deceive ourselves?—'twas so,
> 'Twas even so—and sorrow for the man
> Who either had not eyes wherewith to see,
> Or seeing hath forgotten. Let this pass,
> Suffice it that a shock had then been given
> To old opinions, and the minds of all men
> Had felt it—that my mind was both let loose,
> Let loose and goaded.
>
> (10.849–63)

But in Wordsworth's poetry, the visionary freedoms into which the narrator may be shocked and goaded cannot replace valuable attachments to the everyday and the ordinary, just as the Leech Gatherer's smilingly repeated explanations remain firm and cheerful in the face of the poet's expectations of some otherworldly message. *The Prelude* therefore goes on to describe the confusion which ensues when the narrator tries to establish through his critique a positive alternative to the institutions in disgrace. A revolutionary re-evaluation of human nature, originating in poetic enthusiasm, becomes incoherent when it tries to justify itself theoretically.

> ...Thus I fared,
> Dragging all passions, notions, shapes of faith,
> Like culprits to the bar, suspiciously
> Calling the mind to establish in plain day
> Her titles and her honours, now believing,
> Now disbelieving, endlessly perplexed
> With impulse, motive, right and wrong, the ground
> Of moral obligation—what the rule,
> And what the sanction—till, demanding proof,
> And seeking it in every thing, I lost
> All feeling of conviction, and, in fine,
> Sick, wearied out with contrarieties,
> Yielded up moral questions in despair...
> (10.888–900)

But Wordsworth's poetic contains its *own* theory, implied by its *literary* placement of Wordsworth's judgement on these topics. That is the theory which this book tries to elicit.

The way in which I read Wordsworth has, of course, its own theoretical background which is implicit rather than explicit throughout the book. I give a brief sketch of it here as a conclusion to this Introduction.

Wordsworth is often regarded now as having lived through a 'crisis of representation' whose implications have only been fully appreciated and described by our own contemporary literary theorists. By 'representation' is meant the power of words to stand for objects in the world, thus making present to us the determining characteristics of things which are absent. The 'crisis', highlighted by all literary theories deriving from Saussurean linguistics, results from the contrary belief that language is a differential system, and that words consequently take their meanings from their relations to other words, without reference to an external world at all. Language is no longer thought to match up to the world, and, as a result, the commonsense distinction between literal usage which does and figurative usage which does not becomes problematic.

In Wordsworth's time, it is true, the philosophical followers of Kant lost faith in the world of things-in-themselves which Kant had postulated as the real cause of objects of scientific knowledge—phenomena, or things as they appear under our forms of knowing them. In the thought of Fichte, Schelling and Hegel the concept of a world external to our experience of it withered away from philosophical disuse. But the other side of the story, not so often emphasised these days, is that the desire for realism remained as strong as before and had to be accommodated within the new phenomenology. Wordsworth's will to realism shows his poetry only able to match the world by being always at a figurative departure from it, and therefore by not matching it. Reality, no longer available as a literal category, has not disappeared but is the description to be given to the kind of existence enjoyed in metaphor. We can only grasp the real by a fluid, imaginative response which shows our awareness that any direct correspondence between our language and the world is impossible. The world, in Wordsworth's *Prelude*, is to be approached, not embellished or transformed, through the figurations produced by what he called imagination.

However, Wordsworth's poetry also redresses an imbalance in many of our contemporary theoretical debates by demonstrating that such crises of representation are never purely epistemological; and this book is largely about the way in which Wordsworth shows how the mind's interchanges with nature come to incorporate the apparently different world of social and political concerns. Love of nature leads to love of mankind. Once the epistemological power of poetry, its metaphorical realism, is conceded, then the plot of the 1805 *Prelude* can be understood. We discover the world of nature in a creative manner analogous to the way in which we construct the artificial environment of social and political reality—the community which claims to define our humanity. Nature and culture are realised by the same imaginative effort, but in different degrees, as Coleridge would have said, leaving open the possibility of conflict. The representation of nature is no longer a straightforward mapping of externals but now involves the self-expression resulting from imaginative response. Questions about any representation of nature, therefore, precipitate other questions about the desirability of having the self, which that representation reveals, itself represented in society and perhaps allowed to criticise existing cultural values. The two meanings of representation—epistemological and political—cannot be separated. The undifferentiated potential which nature represents for the child in the 'spots of time' of the 1805 *Prelude* has to be weighed against the standards of what would later constitute an acceptable political or institutional provision for this potential. Epistemological difficulties in recovering memories intact merge with other embarrassments. The political interest is therefore served, as I suggested earlier, by weakening practically or poeticising the representation of any embarrassing excess of significance—embarrassing, that is, to fulfil politically and realise in existing social practices.

This exhibits a caution increasingly characteristic of British reactions to the French Revolution, both favourable and unfavourable. In a book on radicalism in the period, the historian H. T. Dickinson records that during the 1790s, members of a radical Society of Constitutional Information in Sheffield, one of many throughout the country, demanded 'equality of representation', immediately adding that they were 'not speaking of that visionary equality of property, the practical assertion of which would desolate the world, and replunge it into the darkest and wildest barbarism'. Wordsworth's poetry provides a genre or discourse in which such 'visionary' impulses can be indulged without raising the fears of implementation which ran through the conservative and most of the radical opinion of his day; not necessarily visions of a classless society, but at least of a mode of self-understanding in nature apparently free of social constraint.

I try to do justice, therefore, to what I take to be Wordsworth's exemplary emphasis on the integration of epistemological and political concerns. I do this rather than try to look for disruptions in his writings caused by a pure textuality: shortfalls in poetic expression resulting from the indeterminate nature of language prior to its saturation in powerful political interests. It is surely right to stress that there is no *use* of words prior to such historical investments. I think this is the fundamental insight of the 1805 *Prelude* in going beyond the 1799 *Prelude* to investigate the purely poetic version of reality not on its own but by means of the analogous socio-political construction, exposing the way in which both are already shaped by belonging to the same ideology. That relationship prescribes limits to the poetic self, gradually trimming its 'miraculous', revolutionary wish to give 'to duty and to truth/ The eagerness of infantine desire' (II, 23–4).

Chapter One

Personal Talk

Most contemporary and many subsequent discussions of Wordsworth's poetry return with unerring regularity to note its characteristically insistent egoism: 'he may be said', as Hazlitt remarked drily, 'to take a personal interest in the universe'. Wordsworth himself admitted of *The Prelude* that 'it seems a frightful deal to say about one's self'. More revealing and helpful, though, is his reformulation of this anxiety a year later in 1805, in terms of the poem's position in literary history: 'a thing unprecedented in Literary history that a man should talk so much about himself'. The personal confrontation which Wordsworth forces on his readers, and which so many of them have resented, is symptomatic of wider historical issues. Wordsworth's originality within the English literary tradition is inseparable from his self-exploration: the fact that much of this was expressed in the first-person singular often obscures for us the unnerving objectivity of his effort. Or, to put it another way: if Wordsworth is to be identified with the 'I' of his poems, the results are not obviously consoling or self-gratifying. In fact

9

they expose a disquieting paradox: in Wordsworth's self-explorations, traditional notions of the personal are those most clearly found to be inadequate.

The idea of what is 'personal' appears to be closely linked to the idea of what is 'private'; but we live in an age in which the idea of privacy has become problematic. Philosophical, psychoanalytical, political and literary theories have repeatedly questioned the coherence of the assumption, going back at least to Descartes, that we have an inner self experienced in opposition to an external world. The language expressive of this private self would be the prerogative of every individual, verifiable only by him or her; but there has been a powerful tendency to construe this language as being parasitical upon or even constructed out of the public discourses which are available at the time. By that is meant that the larger forms out of which our identities are shaped are unique to none of us, bearing only the stamp of our historical period, culture and social milieu. Major thinkers as different in intellectual commitment and approach as Marx, Freud and Wittgenstein have contributed influentially to this movement which goes back to the Romantic individualism against which it is often taken to be reacting. And close to the heart of that is the Wordsworthian egoism which pursues self-definition into realms where the notion of the personal seems to have little place.

The childhood Wordsworth is famous for trying to remember is not only mysterious to his later self, but is presented as being unfathomable at the time. In 1843 Wordsworth dictated a series of notes on his poems to Isabella Fenwick. He had this to say of his 'Ode: Intimations of Immortality from Recollections of Early Childhood':

> I used to brood over the stories of Enoch and Elijah, and almost to persuade myself that, whatever might become of others, I should be translated, in something of the same way, to heaven.

With a feeling congenial to this, I was often unable to think of external things as having external existence, and I communed with all I saw as something not apart from, but inherent in, my own immaterial nature. Many times while going to school have I grasped at a wall or tree to recall myself from this abyss of idealism to the reality. At that time I was afraid of such processes. In later periods of life I have deplored, as we all have reason to do, a subjugation of an opposite character, and have rejoiced over the remembrances...

One might have expected that a sense of self, encompassing all external things, would foster a feeling of security: the child could not feel alienated from a world which was part of himself, and his self-consciousness would have the solidity and permanence of natural objects. Yet the abyss begins to open up in front of him in proportion to his selfish appropriation of the world. With the increase in self-consciousness comes an uncertainty of self-definition. Like Narcissus, he finds that as the world becomes self-contemplation, it also becomes ungraspable.

Wordsworth, though, is also claiming that in later life we deplore the oppressive reality of the external world. He wants, that is, to recall the abyss within himself and recover what he goes on to call the 'dream-like vividness and splendour which invest objects of sight in childhood'. This would be to apprehend the world as dream—the insubstantial, symbolic end of a relation which has its original elsewhere, in this way intimating a region beyond mortality. We should note the connection for Wordsworth between finding nature symbolic, and feeling it as an extension of himself. His experience grows progressively more poetic and unreal to the extent that it moves beyond the traditional boundaries of individuality separating the private and the public, the inner and the outer. Wordsworth's originality as a poet, his newness in 'Literary history', results from his talk 'about himself' in a way which makes us forfeit our literal

expectations of this self as a person. In the language of the
'Immortality Ode', he can only become conversant with the
'Soul's immensity', our 'best Philosopher' and 'Mighty
Prophet', if he also becomes 'a little child'.

The sonnet was praised by Wordsworth (in a sonnet
written in 1827, 'Scorn not the sonnet...') as the most
economical vehicle of poetic self-expression, perfected in
English by Spenser, Shakespeare and Milton. It is with
Miltonic assurance that Wordsworth meets head-on the
paradoxes resulting from his original talk about himself in
the first of a series of sonnets first published in 1807 and
eventually entitled 'Personal Talk':

> I am not One who much or oft delight
> To season my fireside with personal talk,
> About Friends, who live within an easy walk,
> Or Neighbours, daily, weekly, in my sight:
> And, for my chance-acquaintance, Ladies bright,
> Sons, Mothers, Maidens withering on the stalk,
> These all wear out of me, like Forms, with chalk
> Painted on rich men's floors, for one feast-night.
> Better than such discourse doth silence long,
> Long, barren silence, square with my desire;
> To sit without emotion, hope, or aim,
> By my half-kitchen my half-parlour fire,
> And listen to the flapping of the flame,
> Or kettle, whispering it's faint undersong.

Here the affront to our expectations of the self-defining
qualities of privacy is at its most calculated. The plain,
domestic setting, contrasting with the transient festivities of
the rich, possesses a deceptive simplicity. The poem homes
in on the permanent features of a subjectivity which are
incapable of being erased: essential characters rather than the
temporary guidelines of pleasurable distraction—the chalk-
marks for the dancers to follow. Yet what remains seems to

be just the opposite of what might be expected to motivate personality:

> Better than such discourse doth silence long,
> Long, barren silence, square with my desire;
> To sit without emotion, hope, or aim,
> By my half-kitchen my half-parlour fire. . .

We can only grasp the nature of this desire when we understand that its squaring leaves it without a defining object, target or end. The fulcrum word 'square', balancing silence and desire, recalls the dance patterns drawn in chalk through its sense of a delimited rectilinear match. But it also suggests the multiplication of a thing by itself, the common mathematical meaning familiar to *The Prelude*'s student who found intellectual relief in studying geometry at Cambridge because, significantly, 'Mighty is the charm/ Of those abstractions to a mind beset/ With images, and haunted by itself' (6.178–80). Again, the connection is made between formal patterning and self-duplication, with the reader left to decide if one is a cure or an incitement to the other.

The effect of the sonnet might be a comically exaggerated puritanism, miming the ageing spinsters it pompously cuts, were it not quite awesome in its confident singlemindedness. The mind in question expands enormously because the only things that square with its desire are indeterminate. The domesticity which one expects to be limiting, a place 'where small experience grows', turns out to be the setting for a sense of self outflanking social definition. The last line insists on this contradiction: 'Or kettle, whispering it's faint undersong'. The word 'it's' has to be stressed, both for the line to scan, and to get full onomatopoeic value— 'undersong'—out of 'whispering'. The particularity of the kettle on the hearth will not let us forget the reclusive, withdrawn, unsociable circumstances required to reveal the larger Wordsworthian personality.

This is only the first of a sequence of four sonnets. In the others, Wordsworth argues that going into retreat is a way of engaging with wider issues: 'Wings have we, and as far as we can go/ We may find pleasure'; but this inner uplift is shown eventually to rest on the more orthodox support of 'the substantial world' of books. 'There do I find a never-failing store/ Of personal themes, and such as I love best;/ Matter wherein right voluble I am'. This seems rather tame in comparison with the uncompromising scepticism of the first sonnet. More in tune with it is the conclusion to another sonnet written around the same time (1802–4), one which Wordsworth described to the diarist Crabb Robinson as being 'of pure fancy'.

> How sweet it is, when mother Fancy rocks
> The wayward brain, to saunter through a wood!
> An old place, full of many a lovely brood,
> Tall trees, green arbours, and ground flowers in flocks;
> And Wild rose tip-toe upon hawthorn stocks,
> Like to a bonny Lass, who plays her pranks
> At Wakes and Fairs with wandering Mountebanks,
> When she stands cresting the Clown's head, and mocks
> The crowd beneath her. Verily I think,
> Such place to me is sometimes like a dream
> Or map of the whole world: thoughts, link by link,
> Enter through ears and eyesight, with such gleam
> Of all things, that at last in fear I shrink,
> And leap at once from the delicious stream.

The fear comes from the dizzying breadth of concern, the 'map of the whole world', revealed as the abyss opens once more and external reality becomes 'like a dream'. This is the fear to which the first sonnet of 'Personal Talk' is impervious. The subsequent trust in books to produce themes, 'personal themes', ends in conventional praise for 'The Poets, who on earth have made us Heirs/ Of truth and pure delight by heavenly lays!'—lines which appropriately found their way onto the memorial to Wordsworth in Westminster Abbey. But this conclusion in public panegyric— a shared, social form—should not be allowed to obscure the private, puzzling void which poetry initially had to cover—a self 'without emotion, hope, or aim'. There, without a saving literariness, language reaches out to its opposite—'Long, barren silence'—in order to find for personality an expression unconstrained by social nicety. Its banality threatens to become revelatory of a totally different order of things, as part of a conspiracy to elevate the private individual's significance above the social. But in doing this, Wordsworth's language does not realise an alternative world, as do the mythologies of Blake's prophetic books or Shelley's visions, and dabbles instead in silence. Since this is impossible to sustain in words, the other sonnets return to a renewed sense of the extent to which identity is bound up with words, just as it is dependent on a community—in this case a poetic one—and the mutual recognition of its members. Finally we hear of the poets, 'Oh! might my name be numbered among theirs,/ Then gladly would I end my mortal days'.

The Philosophic Mind

In *The Convention of Cintra*, published in complete form in 1809, Wordsworth remarks that:

> while Mechanic Arts, Manufactures, Agriculture, Commerce, and all those products of knowledge which are confined to gross—definite—and tangible objects, have, with the aid of Experimental Philosophy, been every day putting on more brilliant colours; the splendour of the Imagination has been fading.

15

At first this reads like Romantic escapism, sounding a retreat from the practical world which the rest of us inhabit to a realm of untarnished imagination, probably somewhere in the Lake District. Inevitably the reality is much more complicated. Wordsworth wrote his pamphlet, *The Convention of Cintra*, to condemn the apparent dereliction of duty by the British forces fighting Napoleon in Spain and Portugal. He was writing in popular support of practical intervention, and against the treaty at Cintra with the French. Had the British leaders, especially the future Duke of Wellington, Sir Arthur Wellesley, continued to support the armed struggle of their allies against the French, they would have continued to administer 'a shock to the enemy's power, where that power is strongest, in the imaginations of men'. The splendour of the imagination is to be restored through political action.

Yet this explanation leaves Wordsworth's opposition of imagination and experimental or empiricist philosophy untouched. There is a philosophical background which sheds light on this, and on the pattern of Wordsworthian thought described so far. The thinker in the empiricist tradition to whom Wordsworth was originally most attracted was David Hartley, a mid-eighteenth-century Dissenter whose followers included the scientist and philosopher, Joseph Priestley, and the radical political theorist, William Godwin. Hartley's main work, *Observations on Man* (1749) offers informal intellectual support to 'Tintern Abbey', much in the way that aspects of Berkeley's philosophy are echoed in Coleridge's poems of the 1790s. However, Hartley's scheme, although founded on an empiricist basis of sensation, records a progress through associated ideas towards identification with an immaterial God. Wordsworth's interest in Hartley highlights how his intellectual history is situated at the peak of a general reaction against empiricism or the 'Experimental Philosophy'. This reaction had a predominantly British target in the sceptical empiricism of David Hume, and a German attack in the writings of Immanuel Kant and his successors, although the British opposition to Hume was not insubstantial. Sketching the new development in the broadest terms, we can say that it constituted a shift from one explanation of how knowledge is possible to another. According to the first, to know something was like seeing an object distinct from oneself. Kant's 'Copernican Revolution', as he called it, stood this explanation on its head. He claimed that, on the contrary, all that we could know was the way in which we experienced the object. The nature of the object itself was beyond our reach, except as the cause of our experience of it. That experience was the shape the world has to take for our knowledge of it to be possible. Nature therefore reflects the character of human understanding; and understanding the world becomes a way of interpreting ourselves. Consciousness and self-consciousness become increasingly difficult to separate, and in the work of the post-Kantian philosophers the distinction disappeared.

This conclusion has obvious affinities with Wordsworth's treatment of nature. Nature can be entrusted with an educative power because the child's discovery of nature is also the uncovering of his own resources: both are united in what the Pedlar of 1798 and the narrator of the 1799 *Prelude* call the 'one life'. Yet Kant also believed that, confronted by the immensity of nature, we can have a sublime sense of ourselves—an experience without obvious educative coherence—just as we can postulate an unknown character for things-in-themselves still beyond the reach of our present scientific definitions. So to discover self in nature, as the boy does in *The Prelude*, is to discover something not entirely under our conceptual control. However, Kant is careful to insist that this experience of sublimity remains an aesthetic one, and does not become a practical judgement on which

17

we might act. Later writers—Schiller in Germany and
Shelley in England—claimed that this larger, aesthetic
apprehension of self was indirectly practical: it urged us to
change the world into a form in which it could be fulfilled.
When Wordsworth argues provocatively that,

> One impulse from a vernal wood
> May teach you more of man;
> Of moral evil and of good,
> Than all the sages can...

he also seems to support a model of self-knowledge in nature
which ostentatiously places itself beyond traditional para-
digms and authorities. The poem is the polemical expression
of a lyrical alternative to systematic philosophy. It evokes an
experience which offers to correct received ideas that equate
human value with inherited hierarchies of knowledge.

At first it seems reasonable to expect that as a consequence of this movement away from empiricism towards
Kantian idealism, nature would have become less alien and
simpler to understand. No longer heterogeneous, it would
greet us with the familiar symbols of our experience. Events
in nature would offer themselves up for moral and
imaginative interpretation; and the strongholds of the
imagination would again regain the vivid natural existence
desired by *The Convention of Cintra*. But what we have seen
happen at the same time as this apparent domestication of
nature is a deepening and complicating of the idea of the self.
The sublime, extra-conceptual self-consciousness turns out
to be a mysterious apprehension, compounded of layers of
memory, association, repression and symbolic displacement
of all kinds. Shakespeare's characters and Milton's visions
were not inferior to Wordsworth's poems in human insight;
the difference is that the possibilities of psychology had
become an explicit theme by the time of Wordsworth, and
were no longer the accidental rewards of a primarily

dramatic or religious purpose. Nature, as the bearer of this psychological interest, becomes enigmatic and obscure just because it has been cast in the role of an expressive and familiar self.

This epistemological story parallels the political uncertainty of a social class which had, in the French Revolution, reshaped the existing social hierarchy into a more accommodating form reflecting its own interests, and then had watched in horror as the process got out of control. At first it was easy to blame excesses and atrocities on the lower orders; but when the violence was directed against the leaders and originators of the Revolution, it must have looked as though the efforts at political redefinition which previously had seemed unambiguously self-enhancing were in reality fraught with a dark, unconscious purpose. This suspicion produced terror at the Terror, and then a reactionary complacency directed against any attempt to see beyond present fears to an improved and enlightened self-consciousness. Towards the end of the two-part *Prelude* of 1799, Wordsworth described this state:

> . . .if in these times of fear,
> This melancholy waste of hopes o'erthrown,
> If, 'mid indifference and apathy
> And wicked exultation, when good men
> On every side fall off we know not how
> To selfishness, disguised in gentle names
> Of peace and quiet and domestic love—
> Yet mingled, not unwillingly, with sneers
> On visionary minds—if, in this time
> Of dereliction and dismay, I yet
> Despair not of our nature, but retain
> A more than Roman confidence, a faith
> That fails not, in all sorrow my support,
> The blessing of my life, the gift is yours
> Ye mountains, thine O Nature.
>
> (II.478–92)

Urged on by Coleridge, he felt it his task to preserve in poetic vision the philosophical link between 'our nature' and 'Nature': a cautionary yet not despairing endeavour. The 'more than Roman confidence', deliberately exceeding the Revolution's typical aesthetic conception of itself in classical republican terms, seeks repose in religious analogy, 'a faith/ That fails not'. But at this point in Wordsworth's writings, morale is to be maintained by the attempt at a poetic recovery and control of that disturbing but enriching encounter with the self writ large in 'Nature', and reflected back to us in all its unthought of complexities.

Forgetting

Wordsworth's unprecedented place in literary history is historically apt. His personal talk reflects the interests of contemporary political and philosophical thought. His introspection reveals sublime possibilities—what Keats, paraphrasing Hazlitt, called 'the Wordsworthian or egotistical sublime'—fraught with difficulties and even terror. He feels forced to concede the extent to which identity is bound up with the old categories which the generosity of his poetic reading of himself in 'Nature' had seemed to supersede. The greatest efforts of the Wordsworthian imagination are in the face of loss; the recovery and salvage they effect of the past, for example, are either consciously symbolic, so as not to disrupt present realities; or else the imaginative effort itself appears to be the only consolation. This consolation is curiously dependent on loss: we have seen Wordsworth's imagination flourish on indeterminacy, his self-defining desires expand when deprived of a specific object. The collapse of these imaginative advantages into the sense of deprivation and frustration is the tragic possibility so often present in his poems.

20

This is evident in perhaps the most moving of his sonnets, written after the death in 1812 of his three-year-old daughter, Catharine.

> Surprized by joy—impatient as the Wind
> I turned to share the transport—Oh! with whom
> But Thee, long buried in the silent Tomb,
> That spot which no vicissitude can find?
> Love, faithful love recalled thee to my mind—
> But how could I forget thee!—Through what power
> Even for the least division of an hour,
> Have I been so beguiled as to be blind
> To my most grievous loss?—That thought's return
> Was the worst pang that sorrow ever bore,
> Save one, one only, when I stood forlorn,
> Knowing my heart's best treasure was no more;
> That neither present time, nor years unborn
> Could to my sight that heavenly face restore.

The word 'heavenly' strives for an otherworldly meaning, a positive alternative to this world, filled with religious certainty. Yet Wordsworth's 'heavenly' figuratively describes the earth-bound delight in his 'heart's best treasure' and insists on the irreparable quality of his loss. Out of this comes the imaginative effort of the poem, scouring 'present time' and projecting 'years unborn' in its desire for recovery. If 'heavenly' could be an otherwordly absolute, there for familiar appropriation, then, similarly, the narrator ought to be gladdened by the thought that the dead are beyond 'vicissitude'. But what makes good theology cannot unseat the existential commitment of the poem. Wordsworth begins another sonnet of this period (1813–14): 'If thou indeed derive thy light from Heaven,/ Then, to the measure of that heaven-born light,/ Shine, Poet! in thy place, and be content'. It is this complacency which is severely examined in 'Surprized by joy'. Here, heaven is the wrong category of object for an imagination which is, by definition, the bearer of loss and vicissitude: an imaginary heaven would be a contradiction in terms. The painful paradox which the poem celebrates ruefully is that it is the ability to *forget*, not to imagine, which makes life something other than 'the worst pang that sorrow ever bore'. Wordsworth's art of memory has been well-canvassed by the critics, his 'power' of forgetting less so:

> Love, faithful love recalled thee to my mind—
> But how could I forget thee!—Through what power
> Even for the least division of an hour,
> Have I been so beguiled as to be blind
> To my most grievous loss?

The striving for imaginative recall is predictable; the forgetting, the complacency, remain the discovery of the poem.

However, it is the act of forgetting which also allows the poet to shine in his place and be content. Once more we are reminded that Wordsworth does not allow the imagination to establish its own set of positives. It is always part of a movement of mind which returns us to the established notions which he thinks ultimately conserve our identity. Yet Wordsworth is obviously fascinated by characters who appear to have to live their lives entirely in terms of loss and lack. We shall see how, in *Lyrical Ballads*, he is imaginatively drawn to try to fill out the lives of those who exist beyond the social order necessary to one's own sense of individuality. Wordsworth's sensitivity to human suffering is clearly sharpened by an imagination which finds in loss and vicissitude its own freedom. Only if we can appreciate the significance of this conceptual connection can we understand the practical and political inaction which so many Wordsworthian narrators display in front of human suffering. Imaginative generosity in the conception of a person involves, for Wordsworth, a sympathy which exceeds the power to help them. The most personal griefs, like those of the Pedlar for Margaret in 'The Ruined Cottage' (later to become Book I of *The Excursion*) are also the most impotent. Wordsworth has the Pedlar admit to the joys of forgetting:

> ...what we feel of sorrow and despair
> From ruin and from change, and all the grief
> The passing shews of being leave behind,
> Appeared an idle dream that could not live
> Where meditation was. I turned away
> And walked along my road in happiness.
>
> (520–5)

The Pedlar, insouciantly abandoning the scene of Margaret's desertion, despair, sickness and death, accepts that his existence cannot permanently be defined by an imaginative engagement with ruin and deprivation. He is no more callous than the narrator of Milton's 'Lycidas' concluding the elegy on the death of his friend with 'Tomorrow to fresh woods and pastures new'. The difference is in the impotent presence of the Pedlar during Margaret's ordeal, coupled with the sense that he is ultimately seeing beyond her individual importance to a wider context. The Christian expansion of 'Lycidas', on the other hand, ensures God's saving concern for the individual. The insight of Wordsworth's Pedlar is one he is credited with in the first version of 'The Pedlar' (1798), to be partly incorporated in 'The Ruined Cottage' and, later still, in the narrator's experience in the 1799 *Prelude*: 'Wonder not/ If such his transports were; for in all things/ He saw one life, and felt that it was joy'. The oneness could hardly have consoled Margaret; it expresses the shallower, more conventional side of the domestication of nature which, I argue, took place in contemporary philosophical thinking. There is a richer, less acceptable gloss on the

23

Pedlar's attraction to the spectacle of a disintegrating fellow being, his fascination for a human significance which he cannot act upon, only contemplate, the mental sustenance he gains from his wise passiveness in the presence of Margaret's misery. It is given by Rivers (Oswald in the published version of 1842), the villain of Wordsworth's tragedy *The Borderers*, which was probably completed by July 1797.

> Action is transitory, a step, a blow—
> The motion of a muscle—this way or that—
> 'Tis done—and in the after vacancy
> We wonder at ourselves like men betray'd.
> Suffering is permanent, obscure and dark,
> And has the nature of infinity.

Rivers murders a man he was tricked into thinking had been the prime agent in a conspiracy to dishonour him. The exact nature of the injury is left unspecified, focussing attention instead on the kind of resentment Rivers feels, which is of suffering a personal slight. His revenge on his detractor restores his self-esteem. When he discovers that the man was innocent, he can only retain his new sense of integrity by claiming that such mistakes no longer matter: he has moved imaginatively into 'a region of futurity/ Whose natural element was freedom'.

Wordsworth happily took Rivers' speech on action out of its context to provide the motto for 'The White Doe of Rylstone', published much later in 1815. Originally it was spoken by an unscrupulous and unpitying man who nevertheless employs a Wordsworthian rhetoric to describe his desire for an enlarged experience:

> In these my lonely wanderings I perceived
> What mighty objects do impress their forms
> To build our intellectual being...
> Henceforth we are fellow-labourers—to enlarge
> The intellectual empire of mankind.

Such contempt for action does not do very well on the stage. *The Borderers* gives pride of place instead to the introspective adventurousness which is so often the subject for exposition and critique in Wordsworth's other poems. Rivers represents for Wordsworth the seductions and terrors of a positive imaginative life—'a Being who had passed alone/ Beyond the visible barriers of the world/ And travelled into things to come'. The Pedlar, on the other hand, represents the conditions under which he is willing to explore imaginative alternatives to the ready-made, expected moral judgement. Hence the Pedlar's saving power to forget, his retreat from sublimity, and his eventual rootedness, as his later incarnation in *The Excursion* makes explicit, not in Rivers' uncompromising radicalism but in a theodicy—a Christian belief that the significance and value we imagine for ourselves beyond our unsatisfying or tragic individual roles is guaranteed by divine plan. In *The Excursion*, the tragedy of Margaret's life gains its strangely uplifting effect on the Pedlar from its power to hone his awareness of the fulfilment she can expect in the life to come. However this religious solution is barely detectable in 'The Ruined Cottage', and, as we shall see, it cannot completely account for the poetic effort of *The Excursion*, despite Wordsworth's subsequent changes, especially those of 1845, in order to make the religious construction sit more easily on the poem. In the later version the Pedlar dismisses Margaret's tale with the aid of 'meditative sympathies [which] repose/ Upon the breast of Faith'. The 1814 *Excursion* retains the explanation of his 'happiness' in terms of the disturbing pattern of Wordsworthian desire, and does not reach for an external, theological resolution. Before it is rescued by Christian faith, the Pedlar's act of forgetting, or turning aside from Margaret's story, is his only psychological defence against Rivers' fearful power to imagine values beyond the practical duties of personal obligation.

Chapter Two

The Silent Apprentice

The process of becoming a great poet was, in Wordsworth's case, largely hidden from his public. *An Evening Walk* and *Descriptive Sketches* were published in 1793 and admired by the young Coleridge and many reviewers. These, however, are apprentice poems. Presumably Wordsworth thought them good before he had anything better to publish. Although he retained them in later collected editions of his works, the growing sense of what he might be capable of as a poet thereafter inhibited rather than encouraged him to publish. Even the 1805 *Prelude* 'seemed to have a dead weight about it, the reality so far short of the expectation'. The 1793 poems contain hints of what is to come, especially in *An Evening Walk* where Wordsworth's sympathies obviously exceed the pedestrian picturesque and gothic conventions through which his environment is filtered to him. But for the most part the mainly topographical verse shows a dutiful assimilation of lessons learned from his immediate predecessors—from Gray, Thomson, Cowper and others who nevertheless produced in Wordsworth a style which, looking back on this period in the 1805 *Prelude*, he wished to call a 'wilfulness of fancy and conceit' (8.521). Had he stayed on in France in 1793 and perished with fellow moderates or Girondins, and not returned to England to serve his poetic apprenticeship, he would, he tells us, have died 'A poet only to myself, to men/ Useless' (10.199–200). His later work, therefore, despite the fact that his revisions of the 1793 poems continue until 1845, presents itself as breaking through the esoteric diction and decorum he had inherited into what he was to claim as 'the real language of men'. At this stage his 'plain imagination and severe' took an anachronistic literary shape: 'wild obliquities' resulting from a knowing conformity 'to the works of art,/ The notions and the images of books', a power from which 'Nothing was safe' (8.511–86).

Yet the poems which establish his originality and topicality, in which he discovers a recognisable style and subject-matter, emerge only in fragments if at all. 'Salisbury Plain' was written in 1793–94 and revised between 1794 and 1799 as 'Adventures on Salisbury Plain'. Only an extract, 'The Female Vagrant', was published in the 1790s. It appeared as one lyrical ballad among many, with no hint of its ambitious wider context. Coleridge, in *Biographia Literaria*, recalled the unforgettable effect of Wordsworth's recitation of the larger poem. Wordsworth eventually published a much altered version in 1842. Another major effort, mostly during the autumn of 1796 and the spring of 1797, produced his tragedy *The Borderers* which, although offered to Convent Garden in December 1797, also remained unpublished until 1842. Finally, 'The Ruined Cottage' and 'The Pedlar', poems which Wordsworth alternately merged and separated, record a creative process which began in 1797 but only reached the public in the first Book of *The Excursion* in 1814. It is one of those earlier versions which Coleridge described in a letter as 'the finest

Poem in our Language, comparing it with any of the same or similar Length'. If, in passing, we remind ourselves that *The Prelude* had its origin in the same material and related fragments but was not published until 1850, it appears impossible for Wordsworth's early audiences to have formed any just estimation of his talent.

These audiences were given *Lyrical Ballads* and its 'Advertisement' in 1798, and then the enlarged volume of 1800 and its 'Preface', without any indication of the work which had led up to these volumes, or the work in progress from which they emerged. They therefore looked deceptively similar to poems appearing in periodicals of the time, and were not obviously part of Wordsworth's continuing poetic examination of 'ten shameful years' (10.178). Now, thanks mainly to the comprehensive texts so far published in the Cornell edition of his works, Wordsworth's readers can follow the significant development which was hidden from all but his immediate circle, and which later was available only to scholars prepared laboriously to sort out and decipher the manuscripts in Dove Cottage.

With so much material at his disposal, Wordsworth's reticence in publishing is remarkable. Immense ambition and extreme fastidiousness might explain his reluctance to consider any version a final form, or more than part of a larger whole. In 1842 Wordsworth was perhaps less of a perfectionist; but his last revisions, and the distance in time, must also have served to remove any lingering political embarrassment over the degree to which some of his work in the 1790s implicates his poetic vision with that of the Revolution in its early stages. His first notable act of self-censorship had been not to publish the letter he wrote in 1793 to Richard Watson, the Bishop of Llandaff, provoked by the Appendix to Watson's sermon 'On the Wisdom and Goodness of God in having made both Rich and Poor'. It seems innocuous now for someone to have objected to remarks of the kind with which Watson opens one of his paragraphs: 'The provision which is made for the poor in this kingdom is so liberal, as, in the opinion of some, to discourage industry'. But Wordsworth's letter goes beyond the obvious reply to this lofty complacency and responds with an apology for the Revolution.

> This apparent contradiction between the principles of liberty and the march of revolutions ... must of necessity confuse the ideas of morality and contract the benign exertions of the human heart. Political virtues are developed at the expense of moral ones.

This is much more extreme than is needed to answer Watson's heartlessness. Its pragmatism embarrassingly anticipates the ideas of Rivers who, in *The Borderers*, also tries to bypass morality in the interests of political progress: 'His imagination is powerful, being strengthened by the habit of picturing possible forms of society where his crimes would be no longer crimes' (Preface, 64). By 1797 Rivers' position is indefensible to Wordsworth: he is, unquestionably, the villain of the piece. However, the resemblance his statements bear to a Wordsworthian rhetoric of self-exploration have already been pointed out. In his Note of 1842, Wordsworth could gloss this dangerous affinity with equanimity: 'sin and crime are apt to start from their very opposite qualities'. It was his 'long residence in France, while the Revolution was rapidly advancing to its extreme of wickedness' which impressed this process upon him. But in 1797 he cannot distance Rivers so easily, however emphatically he may repudiate him. In his Preface to the play of that year he concedes:

> yet his thirst after the extraordinary buoys him up, and supported by a habit of constant reflexion he frequently breaks

29

out into what has the appearance of greatness; and in sudden emergencies when he is called upon by surprise and thrown out of the path of his regular habits, or when dormant associations are awakened tracing the revolutions through which his character has passed, in painting his former self he really *is* great.

He 'really *is* great' when he is almost indistinguishable from the Wordsworth who also traces 'the revolutions through which his character has passed' by 'painting his former self'. Wordsworth admits in advance the resemblance of Rivers' speeches to the language he will adopt for his own attempts to justify his sense of himself as a great poet.

Rivers' relationship with Mortimer is an attempt at self-recreation which also parodies a major Wordsworthian preoccupation. Rivers wants Mortimer to be tricked into committing a great crime, but in good faith, so that he too will see the absurdity of existing moral conventions, and will join Rivers in reaching imaginatively beyond them. ''Tis slavery—all is slavery, we receive/ Laws, and we ask not whence those laws have come./ We need an inward sting to goad us on.' In poems like 'Tintern Abbey', *The Prelude* and the 'Immortality Ode', Wordsworth is also concerned to justify in poetry sublime emancipation experienced in life. Rivers, as Wordsworth allows, speaks great poetry, whatever else he does. In poem and dramatic character Wordsworth internalises the political debate. That is, the poet interprets on his *own* professional terms the revolutionary urge to move beyond received moral and cultural categories. At the same time, he also removes the question from the practical, political debate. He displaces it by discussing something else: the justification of a poetic afflatus which, by definition, is never a permanent, positive alternative to ordinary experience. In poetry, Rivers can be given his head.

The Borderers shows for the first time the definitive mould in which contemporary political events cast the Words-

worthian imagination. The play is often read as a critique of
Godwinism, the popular interpretation of William Godwin's
widely read *An Enquiry Concerning Political Justice* (1793),
rather than as a response to recent history. In his *Enquiry*,
Godwin produced a theory which predicted the necessary
withering away of all the institutional apparatus of the state
as people became progressively more rational. However, a
considerable part of the education supposed to lead
inevitably to this rational and utilitarian anarchism was the
implantation of an idea of the advantages of Godwin's
scheme. Paradoxically, Godwin's philosophy was both
necessitarian and programmatic: it described what was
bound to take place, provided its principles were adopted.

This ambiguity helps explain how *The Borderers* was both
part of an abstract theoretical debate and an interpretation of
the real events of the French Revolution. Godwinism, in its
hostility to institutions, does represent the Revolution, but
under a description in which the Revolution no longer serves
the interests of the bourgeoisie. Otherwise, Godwinism is a
non-threatening theory of political gradualism: it's all going to
happen necessarily anyway for the best, so no action need be
taken other than to disseminate this idea of human
perfectibility. On the more radical interpretation, though,
Godwinism explains why it cannot be assumed that the
Revolution will gain the equality desired by the propertied
and middling classes and stop there, but on rational grounds
may continue to engineer social parity between all classes. At
this point liberals like Wordsworth, sensing the abyss, are
compelled to argue that Godwinism must be tendentious
rather than necessitarian, programmatic rather than descriptive, partisan rather than scientific and so as self-seeking as
Rivers. To deny that Godwin's theory fits the facts of the
Revolution becomes an ideological imperative.

However, the poetic attractions of the Godwinian challenge
and the apparent symmetry between poetic imagination and

31

Godwinian hypotheses remain undeniable. According to the philosopher Don Locke, 'Godwin is regarded still as the supreme fantasist of reason'. All that the duped hero of *The Borderers* can hope for at the end is the 'forgetfulness' which sustains so many Wordsworthian narrators. There is no suggestion in his letters that Wordsworth was anything other than disappointed when the play was turned down by Convent Garden. The fact that it is the villain Rivers, the rational fantasist, who carries the burden of greatness throughout the play is not compromisingly subversive but tragic. Tragedy is the literary category which makes the inseparability of greatness and weakness, virtue and vice, an inalienable feature of human nature, and so not something which can be changed or reformed. *The Borderers* anticipates the tragic vocabulary Wordsworth applies to events in France in Book 10 of *The Prelude*. It also stands at the midpoint between the straightforward radicalism of the author of 'A Letter to the Bishop of Llandaff' and the 'Salisbury Plain' poems, and the more complicated humanism of the later work.

Late in the summer of 1793, Wordsworth walked across Salisbury Plain. After returning from France the previous autumn, he had lived in London with his brother. Britain and France had been at war since February, and Wordsworth was now cut off from his lover and their daughter, Anne-Caroline, born in December 1792. She was the child of his affair with a French girl, Annette Vallon, from whose story he was in life compelled to turn aside. We can only guess at the future the relationship might have had in more propitious circumstances; no doubt Wordsworth did. Certainly, the guilt and bitterness of the long poem he loosely based on his ramblings across Salisbury Plain is expressed, appropriately, in its indictment of the effects of war, and in its pity for the derelicts, often women, with whom war appears to have populated the Plain. There is a directness in Wordsworth's new treatment of his historical circumstances which does contrast with the discreet eclecticism of his published work. At first this may not have been intended. The first version, 'Salisbury Plain' (1793-94), is Spenserian in versification, but clotted with moralising in ungainly personifications. The passage to become the female vagrant's tale is far from being the 'artless story' it is claimed to be. The war in question is the American War of Independence, one which even Burke thought justified. The fact that the American War, in which Britain was the unjust aggressor, is substituted for contemporary miseries shows the strength of Wordsworth's controversial condemnation of the current war with France. The opening invocation of the savage's 'naked and unhouzed' state is in order to say with Rousseau, and in keeping with a prominent strain of eighteenth-century radical primitivism, that things have got worse. The vicinity of Stonehenge is not to add the gothic *frisson of An Evening Walk*, but to suggest the perception, shared by Isaac Rosenberg in the Great War over a hundred years later, that he was living in 'the same old Druid time as ever', an age of unjustifiable human sacrifice.

Wordsworth began revising 'Salisbury Plain' soon after he had settled with his sister Dorothy at Racedown in Dorset, in 1795. He considered publishing 'Adventures in Salisbury Plain', as it was now called, in 1796, before abandoning it, apart from some final revisions in 1798-99, in order to take up other major projects. In the later poem, the moralistic commentary has mostly given way to a trust in the power of successive narratives to speak for themselves. At the start, the traveller speaks to an old man he meets on the edge of the Plain as though they are characters in a ballad.

'And dost thou hope across this Plain to trail
That frame o'ercome with years and malady,
Those feet that scarcely can outcrawl the snail,
These withered arms of thine, that faltering knee?

Come, I am strong and stout, come lean on me.'
The old man's eyes a wintry lustre dart,
And so sustained he faced the open lea.
(*Adventures*, 10–17)

The old man tells 'how he with the Soldier's life had striven/
And Soldier's wrongs'. The traveller finds him a place on a
passing mail-coach, and next we hear the story of his own
involvement in the war as a sailor, of the government's
failure to pay him, and of the despairing murder he is driven
to commit as a result. The weather forces him to take shelter
in a 'Spital', where he encounters a female vagrant who soon
tells her own tale of sufferings as a camp-follower of war.
What most distresses her is the recollection that she has her
'inner self abused,/Foregone the home delight of constant
truth'. Like other characters, she now is nothing more than
the traumatic tale she tells.

—She ceased, and weeping turned away,
As if because her tale was at an end
She wept; —because she had no more to say
Of that perpetual weight which on her spirit lay.
(*Adventures*, 555–9)

Her story also impresses on its audience, the sailor, a sharper
realisation of his own guilt; but the primary effect of the
poem is, as Wordsworth claims in a letter of 1795, to show
that these are creatures of the times, and that there therefore
must be remedies to the ills it describes: 'partly to expose the
vices of the penal law and the calamities of war as they affect
individuals'. The qualification of 'partly' leaves the way open
to tragedy, but the emphasis is still on reform, deploring in
conclusion: 'Those who of Justice bear'st the violated name!'
The sailor meets his dying wife and is moved to give himself
up to the law the poem attacks. His death achieves nothing.

They left him hung on high in iron case,
And dissolute men, unthinking and untaught,
Planted their festive booths beneath his face;
And to that spot, which idle thousands sought,
Women and children were by fathers brought;
And now some kindred sufferer driven, perchance,
That way when into storm the sky is wrought,
Upon his swinging corse his eye may glance
And drop, as he once dropp'd in miserable trance.

(*Adventures*, 820–9)

The pun on 'drop'—the part of the gallows which falls from under the feet of those to be hanged—neatly catches the self-perpetuating character of the violence which Wordsworth has been attacking in the domestic and the foreign policies of his society. The expression of guilt and sorrow, the eye dropping in remorse, can only mime another officially sanctioned brutality.

In the 1842 version, called 'Guilt and Sorrow', the sailor is not hanged: 'Reader, forgive the intolerable thought,' demurs Wordsworth in parenthesis. Up until 1799 the female vagrant is allowed her despairing cry (also excised later); 'Oh! dreadful price of being to resign/ All that is dear *in* being!' At this stage Wordsworth seems sure that he is not describing an inherent feature of the human condition, but its temporary distortions. He is less definite about the kind of poem he is writing. The characters—old man, sailor, female vagrant, the quarrelling family, the cottagers, the sailor's wife—are, apart from the last, not significantly connected within any single narrative or dramatic structure. They are symptoms rather than causes: their meetings are not part of a plot; each has a tale to tell, but each tale is not an integral part of the larger tale which is the poem. At most, the tales are united as the series of clauses in an accusation which the sailor feels as an indictment of guilt, but which the reader is led to transfer to the sailor's society.

Wordsworth is not entirely happy with this Chaucerian latitude. In a letter of 1799 he is already planning, somewhat grudgingly, a more obvious unity.

> Now by way of a pretty moving accident and to bind together in palpable knots the story of the piece I have resolved to make [the female vagrant] the widow or sister or daughter of the man whom the poor Tar murdered. So much for the vulgar. Further the Poets invention goeth not. This is by way of giving a physical totality to the piece...

This uses the rather hopeless, or 'vulgar', remedy of coincidence. *The Prelude* is a poem in which events are unified by the value which they bear to an overall psychology, the biography of a single mind—as would have been the case if the sailor's responses had been the controlling subject of 'Adventures'. The tales in *The Excursion*, on the other hand, to which 'The Ruined Cottage', Wordsworth's next long poem, eventually contributes, are valued for their cumulative effect. The 'stream of tendency' they reveal is not 'a physical totality' but an unfinished sequence—'the procession of our fate'. Miscellaneous tragedies merge in an increasingly religious perspective, unaffected by individual differences.

Wordsworth's major unpublished poems in the 1790s chart the movement in his thought from an outspoken radical criticism of social inequity, through a tragic acceptance of human suffering, towards the calm of religious consolation. The 'Salisbury Plain' poems, the tragedy of *The Borderers* and 'The Ruined Cottage' are nothing like as doctrinaire as parts of the 1814 *Excursion*, but in formal construction 'The Ruined Cottage' anticipates the later solution. It has the loose grouping of characters—the traveller, the Pedlar, Margaret—reminiscent of the 'Salisbury Plain' poems, without the sense that their tales contribute to

a common political indictment. Only the history of
Margaret's 'affliction in the plague of war.... A time of
trouble' (136–54) matches the needless sufferings portrayed
in the earlier poems. There Wordsworth progressively
effaced the stance of moralising narrator, and marshalled his
stories like a list of self-evident charges against his
government. The manuscripts of 'The Ruined Cottage'
record a movement in the opposite direction as Wordsworth
tries to integrate the Pedlar's philosophising more happily
with the tale of Margaret. Her history is satisfactorily defined
neither as political homily nor as self-sufficient tragedy.
When she dies, a hospitable individual has given way to a
burgeoning, interesting, unpretty natural scene.

> She is dead,
> The worm is on her cheek, and this poor hut,
> Stripped of its outward garb of household flowers,
> Of rose and sweet-briar offers to the wind
> A cold bare wall whose earthy top is tricked
> With weeds and the rank spear-grass. She is dead,
> And nettles rot and adders sun themselves
> Where we have sate together while she nursed
> Her infant at her breast. The unshod Colt,
> The wand'ring heifer and the Potter's ass,
> Find shelter now within the chimney wall
> Where I have seen her evening hearth-stone blaze
> And through the window spread upon the road
> Its chearful light.
>   (103–16)

Her dying has taken the form not of tragic self-expression
but of a gradual loss of identity in nature. The ruined cottage
and its overgrown garden cease to symbolise Margaret's
decline, and gradually and literally assimilate her. After the
deaths of her children, her desultory questioning of passers-
by for news of the husband who has inevitably deserted her

37

for the French Wars is all that can rouse her from her torpor.
Yet even this hope only identifies her more completely with a
sense of place:

> Yet still
> She loved this wretched spot, nor would for worlds
> Have parted hence; and still that length of road
> And this rude bench one torturing hope endeared,
> Fast rooted at her heart, and here, my friend,
> In sickness she remained, and here she died,
> Last human tenant of these ruined walls.
>
> (486-92)

We know what to think of Rivers because of conventional
expectations raised by the tragic format in which his
ambitions are presented. Margaret's suffering is not obviously significant, and requires the Pedlar's interpretation
to make it so.

> 'It were a wantonness and would demand
> Severe reproof, if we were men whose hearts
> Could hold vain dalliance with the misery
> Even of the dead, contented thence to draw
> A momentary pleasure never marked
> By reason, barren of all future good.
> But we have known that there is often found
> In mournful thoughts, and always might be found,
> A power to virtue friendly; were't not so,
> I am a dreamer among men, indeed
> An idle dreamer. 'Tis a common tale,
> By moving accidents uncharacms,
> A tale of silent suffering, hardly clothed
> In bodily form, and to the grosser sense
> But ill adapted, scarcely palpable
> To him who does not think.'
>
> (221-36)

We are now dealing with an entirely Wordsworthian mode of writing which we have to be told how to read. It lacks the 'moving accidents' of tragedy, describing instead the progress of an individual beyond normal criteria of identity, beyond her 'bodily form' as she becomes 'scarcely palpable' to our 'grosser sense' amongst so much that is. What those who 'think' gain from her tale is not immediately clear, except that, like the Pedlar, they are not to despair. The reader's interest shifts from Margaret to the Pedlar's response just as his attention had moved from her personality to her environment without—and this is the achievement of the poem—appearing to change the subject. But the Pedlar's feelings are contradictory and express an enigma from which only religion could rescue him, although it is not allowed to do so yet. In the last passage quoted, it is by finding 'reason', 'future good' and 'power to virtue friendly' in Margaret's story that the Pedlar reassures himself that he is not 'a dreamer among men—indeed/ An idle dreamer'. Yet we have already seen that it is precisely his power to find Margaret's fate 'an idle dream that could not live/ Where meditation was' that shows his consolatory power to 'think'; both 'dream' and, as we shall see in *Lyrical Ballads*, 'idleness' are bound up with Wordsworth's idea of poetic perception. In the conclusion added in 1799, the Pedlar forgets Margaret, and his attention finally rests contentedly on the image of nature with which the poem has progressively replaced her: 'those very plumes,/ Those weeds, and the high spear-grass on that wall,/ By mist and silent rain-drops silver'd o'er' (513–15). However the poetry itself has to carry an immense power of lyrical persuasion which will silence the less absentminded reader's demands to hear the reason, promise and moral good the Pedlar had anticipated deriving from Margaret's hopeless saga.

Wordsworth is at last out on his own. No obvious political programme or inherited literary conventions advise his readers what to expect. His poetic originality has grown to cover an inability to subscribe wholeheartedly to practical remedies, and has expanded enormously in the process. It is a huge burden of significance for poetry to sustain on its own, hence Wordsworth's frequent questioning of his own poetic powers: he demanded so much of them. His poetic practice generates those ambitious claims for poetic significance which, probably under Coleridge's influence, he cast in theoretical form in the Prefaces to *Lyrical Ballads* of 1800 and 1802. There he rationalises poetry's semiotic status: the power it arrogates to itself from other forms of writing—political, scientific, literary, religious. Poetry is 'the breadth and finer spirit of all knowledge ... the impassioned expression which is in the countenance of all science'. But it is in such moments as the Pedlar's meditative, lyrical circumvention of understandable demands for explanation, for the moral of his tale, that Wordsworth tries to earn for poetry the right to the grandiose titles of the Prefaces: 'that sublime notion of Poetry which I have attempted to convey'. On the other hand, the systematic tendency with which he supports poetry in *The Excursion* also inevitably weakens it, undermining its centrality by implying that there are some authorities to which it must give precedence, some explanations which it cannot replace.

Chapter Three

Experiments

The nature of the relations between literature and society will always be a controversial subject. For a start, the word 'between' is a misnomer. Literature is an institution, one among many; and people's views about literature will be determined by the authority it ought to enjoy over, or the deference it ought to pay to, the other institutions among which it takes its place—legal, political, religious, educational, and so on. Literature may either support or criticise the ideology behind the other cultural establishments; that is obvious enough. But the force that its criticism can have is still controlled by the institutional status of its own *literary* presentation. This either allows the criticism a freedom which makes it more biting; or else it automatically implies that such criticism, because it is literary, is fundamentally unserious: the more it protests its reforming zeal, the more legible become the signs of a conventional poetic licence. This ambiguous effect of literature's power to internalise and transform a society's view of itself is even more a feature of *Lyrical Ballads* than it was of *The Borderers* and 'The Ruined Cottage'.

41

In the Advertisement to the first collection of *Lyrical Ballads* in 1798, Wordsworth deliberately tried to raise his readers' consciousness of their expectations of poetry: what a piece of writing has to do to qualify as 'Poetry, a word of very disputed meaning'. He thinks that the institution of poetry, poetry with a capital P, may get in the way of people's appreciation of his poems. To remedy this he advances both a conservative and a radical argument.

First of all, his poems recover a tradition more venerable than the fashionable 'gaudiness and inane phraseology' which his readers may anticipate.

> It will perhaps appear to them, that wishing to avoid the prevalent fault of the day, the author has sometimes descended too low, and that many of his expressions are too familiar, and of not sufficient dignity. It is apprehended, that the more conversant the reader is with our elder writers, and with those in modern times who have been the most successful in painting manners and passions, the fewer complaints of this kind he will have to make.

Wordsworth's 'elder' tradition has been shown by scholars to draw on many sources. A list of influences would include, as well as the ballad writers, the more recent poets Thomson, Akenside, Beattie, Cowper and Burns. His interest in ballads would be stimulated by collections such as the one creatively edited by Thomas Percy, *Reliques of Ancient Poetry*, and the translations by William Taylor of modern German ballads by the poet Bürger, such as 'Lenore' and 'The Chase'. He would find his emphasis on passionate simplicity justified in the writings on aesthetics of Hugh Blair and other theorists of the Scottish Enlightenment; and he would see it practised in much magazine poetry of his day. His sophisticated and ironic manipulations of those poems' simple narrative schemes show that he had learned from Sterne's *Tristram*

Shandy to produce results which look forward to the techniques of Browning's dramatic monologues.

Yet no matter how successfully scholarship manages to place *Lyrical Ballads* in context, it cannot ignore Wordsworth's insistence on the radical, experimental character of the collection.

> The majority of the following poems are to be considered as experiments. They were chiefly written with a view to ascertaining how far the language of conversation in the middle and lower classes of society is adapted to the purposes of poetic pleasure. Readers ... should not suffer the solitary word Poetry, a word of very disputed meaning, to stand in the way of their gratification.

'Experiments' is a word from the language used to attack the supporters of the French Revolution. It associates with 'projector', 'speculator' and 'empiric' in a vocabulary of condemnation which has its roots in the conservative thought of Swift and the Augustans and owes its revival to the polemics of Edmund Burke. Thus, Rivers, 'a daring and unfeeling empiric', tries 'to embody in practical experiments his worst and most extravagant speculations'. It is the word 'experiments' which sounds a subversive note in the otherwise innocuous introduction of a lower class of diction, not even dialect, which is still capable of putting the institution of 'Poetry' into question. Wordsworth's modest proposal apparently needs to be hedged with disclaimers of its revolutionary potential which allude, through Sir Joshua Reynolds, to an academic cultural establishment based on familiarity 'with the best models of composition'. Wordsworth's critique of 'Poetry' is from the inside.

Lyrical Ballads renews Wordsworth's investigation of poetry's power to accommodate new vistas opened up by recent history: 'France standing on the top of golden hours,/ And human nature seeming born again' (6.353–4). The

French Revolution was a triumph for a particular social class, the bourgeoisie who forcefully emancipated its conception of itself from the prescriptions of the traditional hierarchy. However, as was noted before, once this liberating process had begun, it was difficult to see where and why it should stop. Of course it did, with the return of the old power structure in the imperialism of Bonaparte and the Restoration of the Bourbons. In the meantime, though, the dangers of an expansionist individualism had been unforgettably impressed on liberal thinkers like the young Wordsworth and Coleridge by the outbreaks of violence in France which became collectively known as the Terror. Yet it was equally arguable that the attempt of the Revolution to free the definition of the human subject from inherited ruling interests had failed because things had not gone far enough. The bourgeoisie rose on the shoulders of the lower orders; but once they had established themselves they naturally made no effort to continue the democratic process. Some British radicals, among them Hazlitt and Jeremy Bentham, were determined to see in Napoleon the legitimate child of the Revolution and the champion of its original aims. Others, like Blake, however favourable initially, soon criticised the Revolution not only for betraying its ideals, but also for being unaware of the limited conception of individual fulfilment built into those ideals in the first place.

From this critical perspective, any threat emanating from the Revolution was soon seen to be the same as that of capitalism. Wordsworth eventually recognised that its revolutionary character had disguised the Revolution's real effectiveness for social change: it promoted the ascendancy of the social class most able to profit from an industrial economy. In the 1835 edition of his *A Guide Through The District of The Lakes*, Wordsworth deplored the decline in local yeomanry, their agrarian way of life and related cottage industries, as the machines and the country mansions of the rising industrial 'gentry' took over. By 1844, when he was writing letters to *The Morning Post* protesting against the projected Kendal and Windermere Railway, he had redescribed the threat to traditional Lakeland society as 'Utilitarianism' and the community threatened as 'a perfect Republic of Shepherds and Agriculturists'. In retaliation, he defended feudal tenures and Tory patronage, anything to halt the 'wealthy purchasers'; but his reactionary stance can still be understood as a response to the degeneration of the revolutionary ideal of 'a perfect Republic' of self-sufficient individuals. The Terror was avoided in England, but at a spiritual cost whose damage Wordsworth's poetry constantly sought to repair.

To appreciate what poetry was taking on if it elected to give us, as Wordsworth wanted it to, new views of human nature and an experimental redefining of the individual, these different reactions to the Revolution have to be kept in mind. The art of *Lyrical Ballads* registers both Blakean dissatisfaction and liberal alienation. On the one hand, Wordsworth shows a distrust of the conventional boundaries of poetic genres, blurring and mixing them to increase the angles and multiply perspectives from which the subject is observed. His problematic combinations of lyric and ballad, tragic and comic, heroic and burlesque, visionary and commonplace reflect a Blakean desire to unseat his audience's complacency concerning the proprieties of each—the belief that one viewpoint automatically excludes the other. The reconciliation of opposites effected in this way, however, was ultimately more Coleridgean than Blakean. His experiment showed that, like Blake, he linked the energy of imagination to political reform. Unlike Blake, though, he never felt driven by his dissatisfaction with the definitions of the individual afforded by the distinct art forms he inherited into an uncompromisingly visionary alternative. Blake's prophetic books try to replace the basic recourses to myth and religion of received tradition. Eventually, he stands outside the practice of polite letters, looking balefully in. *Lyrical Ballads* is experimental, certainly, but with a Burkean reservation about the propriety of experiment, and with a commitment to restore rather than replace 'the wardrobe of a moral imagination' which, in Burke's defence of the *ancien régime*, had grown rather shabby. In his 'Essay on Morals', also written in 1798, Wordsworth objected to moralists like William Godwin who 'attempt to strip the mind of all its old clothing when their object ought to be to furnish it with new'. For Blake, perhaps, there was, in Yeats' phrase, 'more enterprise in going naked'; but Wordsworth is happy with the conserving Burkean metaphor, although eager to re-animate it by application to characters and social groups scarcely considered by Burke to be of exemplary interest.

This is because Wordsworth remains equally sensitive to that reading of the Revolution which emphasises the disastrous consequence of an unrestrained attempt to expand the terms of definition of the individual. He therefore prefers to revamp, or force into unusual co-operation, traditionally discrete, individual modes of poetic understanding. Or else he links the desire for an even larger articulation of the self with death, over a hundred years before Freud's shocking marriage of the pleasure principle to the death wish. Wordsworth achieves this by investing *nature* with the authority of the visionary imagination to exceed inherited cultural restraints in the articulation of the self.

Blake dismissed this identification of vision and nature as an excuse for restricting the power of imagination. According to his remark in the margins, in Wordsworth's *Poems* of 1815 we see 'the Natural man rising up against the Spiritual Man'. But we have to recognise how usefully the brake which nature applied to pure vision served to express Wordsworth's ideological position. In imagination Wordsworth could identify a character's possibilities, or the momentousness of his or her value to a narrator, with the larger process of nature. Such exaggerations ensured the desired expansion of personal significance, but only on pain of dissolution or death. We are not wholly seasonal creatures: the winter of our lives is followed by no spring; our identities as persons cannot survive an unlimited natural extension. Wordsworth is drawn frequently to push the narrator's definition of a cherished individual paradoxically beyond his reach. Margaret, Lucy, the Danish boy, the boy of Winander and Wordsworth's own childhood only enjoy celebration in poetic imagination at the expense of personal coherence, as do those afflicted with the lesser deaths of madness ('their lives are with God,' Wordsworth told Isabella Fenwick) and the gentle subsidence into natural processes which Wordsworth attributes to the quiescence of senility. His act of holding up these characters as examples of a larger self-fulfilment, gained through a greater intimacy with a nature beyond political classifications, reveals them also to be in some fundamental way alien, irrecoverable, lost or dead. The elemental significance which Lucy achieves, 'Rolled round in earth's diurnal course/ With rocks and stones and trees', forfeits the relative simplicity, the 'thingness' of a personality taken for granted. Enhancing the definition of the individual to this cosmic extent becomes indistinguishable from annihilating it.

Wordsworth's choice of poetic subjects cannot help implying that those who are in some way socially disabled or disinherited are especially qualified to be the bearers of an uncensored imagination. The complexity of his portraits is to suggest at the same time that the inheritance of social restraints and inhibitions cannot be given up. He typically tries to occupy both positions at once; welcoming as 'genuine inmates of the household of man' characters whose individuality, he has managed to show, consists in living outside the community. He creates a radical distance between poetry and

47

ideology, between his imagination and the traditionally accredited sources and representatives of imagination. It is only finally that one realises that he has thought of this separation as being internal all along; the ideological commitment was never really in doubt. Paradoxically, the effect of his sympathetic efforts to render their integrity has shown his outcasts to be mad, dead, senile, or in some less dramatic way unassimilable. At the end of many of these poems we feel like Timothy in 'The Childless Father', closing his door on an empty privacy.

In *Lyrical Ballads* Wordsworth usually describes as dream-like or visionary those moments when nature takes on responsibility for personal articulation. Dream and vision become qualities of natural perception, not alternatives to it, a partnership receiving most confident expression in the Prospectus to *The Excursion* and most fraught defence in the 'Immortality Ode', as we shall see. But years earlier Wordsworth had implied uncertain or pessimistic conclusions to his natural vision. In 'To Joanna', the girl's laughter is taken up by her echoing surroundings and lent a visionary reduplication.

> Now whether, (said I to our cordial Friend
> Who in the hey-dey of astonishment
> Smil'd in my face) this were in simple truth
> A work accomplish'd by the brotherhood
> Of ancient mountains, or my ear was touch'd
> With dreams and visionary impulses,
> Is not for me to tell; but sure I am
> That there was a loud uproar in the hills.
> And, while we both were listening, to my side
> The fair Joanna drew, as if she wish'd
> To shelter from some object of her fear.

This is a fearful expansion of the human voice into something alien, something which contrasts with the

48

defining kinship, the affectionate trust which draws Joanna to the narrator and is commemorated by the poem.

'There was a boy', later included in the 1805 *Prelude*, is even more pessimistic about the ultimate benefits of an aesthetic education received in imaginatively identifying with nature:

> ...he, as through an instrument,
> Blew mimic hootings to the silent owls
> That they might answer him. And they would shout
> Across the wat'ry vale and shout again
> Responsive to his call, with quivering peals,
> And long halloos, and screams, and echoes loud
> Redoubled and redoubled, a wild scene
> Of mirth and jocund din. And, when it chanced
> That pauses of deep silence mock'd his skill,
> Then, sometimes, in that silence, while he hung
> Listening, a gentle shock of mild surprize
> Has carried far into his heart the voice
> Of mountain torrents, or the visible scene
> Would enter unawares into his mind
> With all its solemn imagery, its rocks,
> Its woods, and that uncertain heaven, receiv'd
> Into the bosom of the steady lake.

The boy's most individualising attention, when we listen to him listening, gradually becomes indistinguishable from his environment. The poetry has to resort to a lyrical evocation of silence, an irony which reflects the ambivalence of the boy's enhanced awareness. He is bound up in an educative exchange which is essentially uncontrollable and will outlast him. Nature answers him, as it does Joanna, by reduplicating his call; but this, and the succeeding invasion of the boy's consciousness by larger natural forms, will eventually outstrip rather than serve his individual interests. His premature death, nature's final infiltration of the merely individual, is again matched by the concluding irony:

Wordsworth's fine lyrical afflatus in response to the challenge of silence collapses in muteness in front of the boy's grave: 'A full half hour together I have stood,/ Mute— for he died when he was ten years old.' Similarly, there is no relationship imaginable in this final togetherness, only the nearness of one minute to the next.

Poems and Narrators

In *Lyrical Ballads*, then, poems which combine traditionally separate forms of self-expression exist side by side with poems which propose a dubious enhancement of the personality of characters by identifying them with a sympathetic nature. Dubious, because ideas which the poems had us think were mutually supportive—individuality and consciousness—turn out to lead in different directions. The two kinds of poem are not always separable, but they represent a useful division for critical purposes. Roughly speaking, the earlier volume of 1798 shows more interest in the first kind, and the enlarged 1800 volume has more of the second.

The *Lyrical Ballads* of 1798 exhibits the mixture of trust and scepticism in Wordsworth's 'experiment': the poet is content to work in existing genres, although bringing them together implies the insufficiency of each. In these poems the consciousness, the inner lives of characters, tend to emerge most strikingly in those moments when readers are made to realise the variety of attitudes which the poem's sympathies require them to adopt. In 'Lines left upon a Seat in a Yew Tree', Wordsworth describes the kind of poet he does not want to be. This character successfully arms his imagination against the diminished views of society in all but one respect.

> He was one who own'd
> No common soul. In youth, by genius nurs'd,

And big with lofty views, he to the world
Went forth, pure in his heart, against the taint
Of dissolute tongues, 'gainst jealousy, and hate,
And scorn, against all enemies prepared,
All but neglect...

Neglect defeats his original purpose, forcing him to accept the public evalution of his 'lofty views', making him listen, unwisely passive, to other voices, 'dissolute tongues' which prevent him from creating the taste by which he ought to be enjoyed. In reaction, his vision becomes eccentric and solipsistic, contemptuous of the shared, public responses which Wordsworth artfully shapes to his own ends throughout the rest of *Lyrical Ballads*. His pride in privacy nourishes a sensibility which strives for its own dissociation.

And lifting up his head, he then would gaze
On the more distant scene; how lovely 'tis
Thou seest, and he would gaze till it became
Far lovelier, and his heart could not sustain
The beauty still more beauteous.

Unlike the rewarding dialectic which Wordsworth was to establish in *The Prelude*, this is a famishing, a feeding on illusory sustenance.

... and so, lost man!
On visionary views would fancy feed,
Till his eye streamed with tears. In this deep vale
He died, this seat his only monument.

His decline into an early grave charts the melodramatic course of heroes of the literature of sensibility whose pretensions were widely criticised in the Romantic period by writers as different as William Godwin and Jane Austen. The deterioration of this man of feeling began with his acceptance of

51

public neglect and his own mirroring of that isolation in a deliberate reclusiveness. Wordsworth's solution, offered in the poem's final lines, describes the pragmatism of *Lyrical Ballads*.

> O, be wiser thou!
> Instructed that true knowledge leads to love,
> True dignity abides with him alone
> Who, in the silent hour of inward thought,
> Can still suspect, and still revere himself,
> In lowliness of heart.

In the other poems, traditional modes of definition, hierarchies and authoritarian stances are there to be suspected; what is to be revered is the character, the subject, the self which appears larger and more compelling for its power to resist complacent, unreflecting descriptions.

When Wordsworth expanded his original Preface for the edition of 1802, he wrote that

> the poet writes under one restriction only, namely, that of giving immediate pleasure to a human Being possessed of that information which may be expected from him, not as a lawyer, a physician, a mariner, an astronomer, or a natural philosopher, but as a Man.

The writer of 'A Poet's Epitaph' reiterates this, dismissing various characters in which a mourner might approach the grave—statesman, lawyer, doctor, soldier, physician, philosopher and moralist. Eventually the proper mourner is identified. Interestingly, he is not described as the poet in all of us, the universal 'Man', but as someone who is himself a professional; someone whose vocation must appear as weakness and escapism in the eyes of others.

> But he is weak, both man and boy,
> Hath been an idler in the land;

Contented if he might enjoy
The things which others understand.

Maybe enjoying what others understand is the humanising
influence ascribed to the poet of the Preface who carries
'sensation into the midst of the objects of the Science itself'.
But the poem's diffident tone is alien to the Preface. 'Idle'
alternatives to work provoke noticeably unstable responses
in the 1800 volume, from Matthew's 'idle songs' to the
narrator's appeal to his sister to enjoy an idle day with him in
the belief that 'One moment now may give us more/ Than
years of toiling reason'. The 'son of Idleness', condemned
along with other 'Tourists' at the start of 'The Brothers',
turns out to be the hero of the poem. In 'The Idle Shepherd
Boys' two lads help save a stranded lamb on their
wanderings. Whether the lamb's peril was due to their
professional neglect or not, they are only gently upbraided
by the poet who assists them, and who is a professional idler:
'one who loves the brooks/ Far better than the sages'
books,/ By chance had thither strayed.'

From Wordsworth's defence of his profession, one would
expect his poetry to be interested in the ways in which the
apparently idle response can embarrass the pretensions of
more professedly serious attempts to understand the world.
A good example is 'We are seven', one of several lyrical
ballads which record a contest between narrator and
character. The narrator's failure to impose his language and
get the character to accept his interpretation of her
behaviour is the poem's success. In 'We are seven', the little
girl, questioned by someone who supposedly knows better,
sticks to her story. Despite the dispersal of her brothers and
sisters—two at sea, two living elsewhere, two dead—they
still 'are seven'. Her sense of kinship is too strong to allow
conventional notions of separation to intrude. Increasingly,
the puzzled narrator's interrogation reveals itself to have

become a desire to dictate the truth:

> 'But they are dead; those two are dead!
> Their spirits are in heaven!'
> 'Twas throwing words away; for still
> The little Maid would have her will,
> And said, 'Nay, we are seven!'

The child is allowed her own language. The poem shifts from confidently correcting irrationality to exposing the competing interests behind differing points of view. The narrator's refusal to accept any answer other than the one he seeks makes us feel less interested in whether the little girl is right or not about her communion with the two dead siblings, and makes us more concerned about her right to hold that point of view. Put under threat, that right appears more and more valuable: something touching on the borderline between the educating adult and the freedom of the child. The narrator is crassly devoted to being the former; the poem is committed, however irresolutely and quizzically, to the latter. The authority one might have expected to remain with the narrator is undermined, and the childish error is left unexplained and irreducible. The poem acknowledges the child's right to speak, but can only do so through the admission that her words cannot be paraphrased.

The irony here is that the poem invokes the autonomous existence of the child by failing to offer a meaningful commentary on her words. A contrast with this poem would be 'The Mad Mother'. Here the kinship is not mysterious: that of a mother for her child. But again this relationship is made strange, our preconceptions of it unsettled:

> I'll teach my boy the sweetest things;
> I'll teach him how the owlet sings.
> My little babe! thy lips are still,
> And thou hast almost suck'd thy fill.

—Where art thou gone my own dear child?
What wicked looks are those I see?
Alas! alas! that look so wild,
It never, never came from me:
If thou art mad, my pretty lad,
Then I must be for ever sad.

We had perhaps forgotten that she was mad, assuming that
Wordsworth's point was rather going to be that in madness
the maternal passion is more naked, more expressive of a
common human nature. But it is this most basic of kinships
which is disturbed by the woman's madness. Being mad,
does she misconstrue her child's looks as 'wicked'? The
sympathies asked for by the poem up to this point certainly
did seem aimed at getting the reader to judge her expressions
as pathetically deranged. If this is so, her influence over the
child may be harmful. Or if the child had *not* inherited her
madness, would his sanity not display itself in just such an
alienation from his mother?—'It never, never came from
me'. To rejoice in the kinship of mother and child seems to
will the child's madness; yet the kinship was the recognisable
bond which enforced our liberal sympathies in the first
place. The poem's conundrums capture the predicament of
the sane who try to enter sympathetically into the lives of the
insane. Madness here is a closed circle which we can only
relate to in bad faith just because it is defined by
misapprehension, disorientation and uncertainty.

The successful evocation of individuality through the
embarrassment of a narrator's conventional approach is
repeated in 'Old Man Travelling'. The poem starts confidently, moving straightforwardly towards a definition of
the old man's singularity.

The little hedgerow birds,
That peck along the road, regard him not.

> He travels on, and in his face, his step,
> His gait, is one expression...

But soon the narrator is forced to qualify, even contradict, his own descriptions in order to render the distinctive impenetrability of his subject. Here one does not encounter the satisfying defeat of an overweening narrator, like that of the combative questioner of 'We are seven'. There is instead a gradual unfolding exploration of the old man's existence in a world beyond ratiocination.

> A man who does not move with pain, but moves
> With thought—He is insensibly subdued
> To settled quiet: he is one by whom
> All effort seems forgotten, one to whom
> Long patience has such mild composure given,
> That patience now doth seem a thing, of which
> He hath no need. He is by nature led
> To peace so perfect, that the young behold
> With envy, what the old man hardly feels.

None of the words sticks. They are as insufficient as the label pinned to the blind beggar Wordsworth saw in London and described in *The Prelude* (7.608–23). In 'Old Man Travelling', the narrator is put in the position of mild detractor: each ascription has to be subsequently withdrawn. Pain is replaced by thought, which is disqualified by 'insensible'; 'patience' and 'peace' cling precariously to the old man, deprived of their usual meanings. Words try to shape his condition with their own precariousness, yet tend to suggest a tough resilience on his part taking over where they leave off.

Descriptions like these are full of a consciousness of the boundaries they imaginatively cross—inner/outer, inanimate/animate, child/adult, sane/mad, polite/rustic. The artistic resources required to make these crossings are part of the subject-matter of the poems. The narrators' apparent abdication of their own authority asks for ironic appraisal. Narrative failings only contribute further to the illusion of the finished roundness of the character outlined by words which can penetrate no further, serving a poetic function which supersedes that of the narrator.

This pattern recurs in other poems in the 1798 volume. In 'The Thorn', the curiosity of the narrator of Martha Ray's tragic story is criticised. Sympathy for Martha, the jilted infanticide, is invoked in spite of rather than through the narrator's prurience: 'credulous', 'talkative' and 'super-stitious', as Wordsworth's Note to the 1800 edition has it, he connives at the fascinated abhorrence emanating from the community which has ostracised her. His refusal to state categorically that Martha has killed the child does not testify to his desire to treat Martha justly and with understanding, but shows his pleasure in preserving the *frisson* of a sensational mystery. All we have, though, are his words: Martha's lament is never allowed to tell a tale. The 'Lyrical and rapid Metre', the Note tells us, is to hold our interest in the mental processes of an unsympathetic narrator, not Martha. The naive lines which brought Wordsworth more critical vituperation than any others he wrote ('I've measured it from side to side:/ 'Tis three feet long, and two feet wide') are, as a result, best read as disingenuous. Most obviously, they comically discredit the language of measure-ment, as useless as the narrator's telescope in a storm: the significance of Martha's tragedy is not something which can be computed or weighed in any simple scales of justice. Also, the lines highlight the way the narrator persists in a confessedly misguided investigation which consequently allows superstition and mystery to go unchallenged: 'I cannot tell how this may be,/But plain it is...'; and, of course, superstition and mystery flourish at Martha's expense.

Similarly, at the end of 'Simon Lee', there is a feeling of revulsion, this time on the narrator's as well as the reader's part, at being confined to the language of one community without being able to formulate a just alternative:

> —I've heard of hearts unkind, kind deeds
> With coldness still returning.
> Alas! the gratitude of men
> Has oftener left me mourning.

The narrator seems momentarily as discontented with moral relationship—gratitude for the good deed of being helped— as Blake might have been, seeing suddenly the oppressive social structure on which his charity feeds. 'You're over-tasked, good Simon Lee...', he says; but the conclusion he draws is one of introspective melancholy: a return upon a self now uneasily richer from recognising a kinship, a common cause, existing beyond and unsatisfied by the ordinary decencies. Yet this new area is never expressed except as present inadequacy.

So it is with 'The Idiot Boy' whose narrative art is the most sophisticated of the 1798 collection. Teasing, patronising and lyrical by turn, the narrator takes the reader through a variety of sympathetic postures towards the retarded child, Johnny. None of them is adequate. His mother, Betty Foy, provides a mock-heroic framework for Johnny's adventurous ride to fetch the doctor for Susan Gale. He is her knight, her chivalric messenger. This both elevates Johnny too much, and diminishes his true importance. His quest soon becomes Quixotic: back to front on his pony, he ceases to be his mother's champion, becoming 'A little idle sauntering thing'. He is lost, and the narrator sets about finding a language which might describe his adventures more realistically. Among the alternatives with which he teases the reader there enters a new seriousness which will explain the words Johnny is allowed 'in his glory' at the end of the poem. Johnny's nocturnal romp possesses a stagey, gothic eeriness. Yet, oblivious to the conventional limits of normal perception, Johnny also symbolises a lost plenitude of apprehension, a dream-like absorption in nature typical of Wordsworthian self-delight. 'And still and mute, in wonder lost,/ All like a silent horseman–ghost,/ He travels on along the vale.'

Part of the poem's ironic mischief is an uncomfortably close parallel between the reader and Johnny. The narrator inveigles us into suspending judgement on Johnny's failings and, without prejudice, trying him out in various roles. By treating Johnny in this way, the sympathetic reader is only consciously re-enacting the idiot boy's unconscious evasion of the rational censorship which normally rules our perceptions. Johnny becomes the reader's humbling approach to a natural intimacy of Wordsworthian richness.

However the narrator still retains a distancing, comic dimension in his descriptions:

> Perhaps, and no unlikely thought!
> He with his pony now doth roam
> The cliffs and peaks so high that are,
> To lay his hands upon a star,
> And in his pocket bring it home.

The immediacy of Johnny's grasp of nature easily collapses into childish wish-fulfilment. His intimacy with his environment distinguishes itself by being beyond the power of words to represent coherently: 'The cocks did crow to-whoo, to-whoo,/ And the sun did shine so cold'. When the narrator professes himself unable to summon inspirational aid adequate to Johnny's capers, this professional defeatism is disingenuous and playful. He can always reassure himself that Johnny's impenetrability is sub-rational (in the sense of inferior, not in the sense of uncensored and at liberty). From this unquestioned certainty he can afford to be generous.

There is no other language in which Johnny's understanding could present a critical alternative to the norm: even to call it understanding is implausible. But Johnny's rearrangement of simple words defamiliarises them and renews a sense of the potential vividness they lose in ordinary usage. To that extent he is a parody of a poet. Stated like this, the treatment of him seems in bad taste, perpetually patronising and ironically amused at his expense; but the concession to Johnny's way of speaking in the last stanza shows his exemplary side uppermost.

> And thus to Betty's question, he
> Made answer, like a traveller bold,
> (His very words I give to you,)
> 'The cocks did crow to-whoo, to-whoo,
> And the sun did shine so cold.'
> —Thus answered Johnny in his glory,
> And that was all his travel's story.

Johnny's jumbled gibberish reflects too accurately on the medley of genres and attitudes in the poem for the narrator's comfort. The poem's variety eats away at the idea of the narrator's detachment and control. Like the madness of 'The Mad Mother', Johnny's disability both defines our contrasting sanity and suggests its limitations. He grows mysterious and tantalisingly different through the same means by which we establish our own estranging certainties. The poem does not allow one to give these up and believe that Johnny's idiocy delivers the individual to an uninhibited, richer life. Yet it does use Johnny as a focus for showing the boundaries within which we unthinkingly perceive our world. Johnny's comic reversals and fey rapport with owls and the moon suggest both the incoherence which would result from stepping outside normality, and the haunting sense of a larger experience, a more 'tuneful concert', which our rational confinement makes us miss. We constitute ourselves as individuals in opposition to Johnny's purposelessness; but we are constantly attracted by ideas of what might lie beyond our strictly constructed integrity.

The mechanics of a lyrical ballad are now in full view. The lyrical element points to the subjective concerns of the poet. Traditionally, lyricism is private, personal expression. Turn that into technical awareness, and you have poems which explore the degree to which the objective, public, balladic element—the otherness of character and story—can draw out the subjective resources of the poet, his sense of self. To do this, the objective element has to be resistant to interpretation, sometimes beyond the pale, provoking an experimental extension of poetic self-consciousness dissatisfied with social norms it cannot quite replace.

Charity

This rather abstract conclusion can be filled out by considering the second type of lyrical ballad more typical of the 1800 volume. These are poems less interested in the feelings arising from incomplete ways of categorising people, and more concerned to reprove morally and socially unconditioned alternatives. They are best approached through 'Lines Written a few Miles above Tintern Abbey', a poem which at first sight seems quite different from the other poems in the 1798 collection. One thing it shares with the others, though, is the mutually defining conflict of subjective and objective elements. 'Tintern Abbey' is a poem of aspiring personal self-sufficiency which, at its magnificent climax, gropes unexpectedly for alternative objective support. The narrator feels consoled for a loss of joy felt 'when first/ I came among these hills' because he can now imagine or hear in nature a larger self with which he can identify. To describe this requires all the resources of poetic rhetoric.

> For I have learned
> To look on nature, not as in the hour
> Of thoughtless youth, but hearing oftentimes
> The still, sad music of humanity,
> Nor harsh nor grating, though of ample power
> To chasten and subdue. And I have felt
> A presence that disturbs me with the joy
> Of elevated thoughts; a sense sublime
> Of something far more deeply interfused,
> Whose dwelling is the light of setting suns,
> And the round ocean, and the living air,
> And the blue sky, and in the mind of man,
> A motion and a spirit, that impels
> All thinking things, all objects of all thought,
> And rolls through all things.

Yet this, it appears, may not be enough.

> Nor, perchance,
> If I were not thus taught, should I the more
> Suffer my genial spirits to decay:
> For thou art with me, here, upon the banks
> Of this fair river; thou, my dearest Friend,
> My dear, dear Friend, and in thy voice I catch
> The language of my former heart, and read
> My former pleasures in the shooting lights
> Of thy wild eyes. Oh! yet a little while
> May I behold in thee what I was once,
> My dear, dear Sister!

The first passage describes something which has been
'taught' and 'learned', and its assurance seems to require us,
if we are to understand these lines, to share in their
privileged mode of seeing and hearing. This raises expectations of access gained to some super-sensible realm, the
guarantee of religious truth; but the language is not
theological, and sets up its own characteristic poetic

dynamism. Cut free from referential ballast (the relation to the world that 'had no need of a remoter charm,/ By thought supplied, or any interest/ Unborrowed from the eye') the thought begins less to soar than to expand. The words 'chasten and subdue' suggest the presence of a doctrine or moral, just offstage, to which 'nature' and 'music' recall us. But the succeeding transition reverses this 'sad', downward spiral of dutiful subjection with a joyful, elevating 'presence' which (the 'And' of 'And I have felt' unexpectedly implies) is continuous with it. The 'elevated thoughts' surprise in their turn by refocusing our upward gaze upon a movement which instead is inward and outward at the same time: 'deeply' clinches the subject's preceding 'sense sublime' and yet is succeeded by the 'interfused' which coopts the entire universe, 'all things', into the triumphant coda. It is this *use* of language which has demonstrated how 'motion' can become synonymous with 'spirit' in 'the mind of man' because the movement of the verse has become its thought. Nature is evoked, not by persuading us that externals are being represented, but in the prolific momentum of the poetry, making us repeatedly revise our readerly expectations and think through subtle shifts in narrative stance. What we took to be introspection turns out to be a peculiarly intimate observation of nature. In other words, showing nature's power to make us think does not distract us from the scene, but is in fact a way of rendering nature's actively mobile reality, a reality which can be shared (as the coopting 'And' insists) but not pictured.

The advance on the thoughtless, animal, unrepresentable ('I cannot paint/ What I then was') pleasures of boyhood is thus supported by a rhetoric whose elevation of thought actually returns it to a similar immediacy. This circularity in the play of imagery is repeated in the shape of the narrative. The visionary achievement of the poem is suddenly undercut by the reversion to earlier, uncomplicated enjoyments, accessible now in the sight of the sister's pleasures. However, the first passage was surely claiming a philosophical advance on 'thoughtless youth' which makes the second passage redundant? Or perhaps the first passage claimed too much, a vision of humanity unconstrained by social distinctions, an undifferentiated 'music'? To identify with 'humanity' on this scale might be to move beyond any coherent notion of individuality. According to the rest of 'Tintern Abbey', the universal 'sense sublime' which grows out of the youthful joy in nature needs perpetual reminding of its individual origins. The subjective, imaginary self needs the objective scene, the Wye valley and the other person, to measure its larger view of things. And the ordinary appreciation of these realities, meticulously detailed and cherished in the opening and closing descriptions, is what Wordsworth obviously cannot do without, however much his narrator protests that he now comes 'With warmer love, oh! with far deeper zeal/ Of holier love'.

The new poems in the *Lyrical Ballads* of 1800 press at the limits of sympathy. Many of them are about charity. Charity is the name given to a generosity beyond the call of social duty. It therefore never criticises social prescriptions of the limits of sympathy, but is the politically uncontroversial description of actions in response to a deeper kinship or 'music'. In 'The Two Thieves', Old Daniel and little Dan, extreme age and youth, are bound together, apparently beyond the reach of social understanding or approval, by their partnership in thievery. Yet the poem goes on to describe how they fit into a benevolent community, broad-minded enough to overlook their petty crimes.

> They hunt through the street with deliberate tread,
> And each in his turn is both leader and led;
> And wherever they carry their plots and their wiles,
> Every face in the village is dimpled with smiles.

They are saved by dotage and infancy—their interchangeable childhoods. We seem to be reading an argument for the social extension of private and familial tolerance and generosity: these characters generate sympathies which override legal sanctions and raise the consciousness of a universal human character.

> Old Man! whom so oft I with pity have ey'd,
> I love thee and love the sweet boy at thy side;
> Long yet may'st thou live, for a teacher we see
> That lifts up the veil of our nature in thee.

However, the unconditioned kinship of this last stanza has just been comically undercut by the preceding information.

> Neither check'd by the rich nor the needy they roam,
> For grey-headed Dan has a daughter at home;
> Who will gladly repair all the damage that's done,
> And three, were it ask'd, would be rendered for one.

Not a collective magnanimity, transcending individual interest, but a daughter's willingness to underwrite any financial losses, ensures the community's goodwill. What then are we to make of the narrator's claims for the instruction in human nature the village receives from the felonious pair? The poem appears not quite in control of its own ironies: unless what is meant is that any poetic sympathy, however disinterested, never steps entirely outside the social order, but in fact covertly relies upon it. But the force of that last stanza cannot be meant to be exhausted by the trite realism of the plot—that a deeper understanding of human nature reveals only a hidden layer of commercial relationships and obscure self-interest.

Other poems about charity are equally ambiguous. In 'Andrew Jones', the generosity of a passing horseman leaves a cripple with two halfpennies in front of him. Andrew Jones steals the money, saying, 'Under half-a-crown,/ What a man finds is all his own.' In doing this, he brings the narrator's curse upon him:

> And *hence* I said, that Andrew's boys
> Will all be train'd to waste and pillage;
> And wish'd the press-gang, or the drum
> With its tantara sound, would come
> And sweep him from the village!

The narrator, this time, gives us no intimations of a universal human character to be intuited in those beyond the social pale—intimations then demystified when shown to have only the shapes permitted by the society they seem to lie outside. Charity in this poem is represented in the figure of the horseman, transient yet unromantic, merely 'Some Horseman who was passing by'. The wider view from which the narrator rebukes Andrew Jones is firmly placed within society. Andrew Jones is just as vulnerable to larger, impersonal forms of social organisation as was the beggar to his refusal of sympathy. Navy and army, press-gang or drum, may either abduct Andrew or possess him by paying another price under half-a-crown, the King's shilling, after which what they find is all their own. The effect of Andrew's swearing, drunken life on his children will be to leave them 'train'd to waste and pillage'—practices in which the army and navy are meant to be expert. Again, one wonders if the poem is in charge of its own ironies, as the armed forces which defend society, and the anarchic effect which Andrew is hated for nurturing, converge alarmingly. The only alternative to Andrew, since he unconsciously encapsulates a politically accepted violence, remains the unsatisfactory horseman of whom we are told nothing.

Wordsworth's most considerable poem about charity, 'The Old Cumberland Beggar', also has a charitable horseman who this time

> ...does not throw
> With careless hand his alms upon the ground,
> But stops, that he may safely lodge the coin
> Within the old Man's hat...

The old beggar receives good treatment wherever he goes. Because he elicits the best in people he is socially useful, and laws which forbid his vagrancy are misguided. Once more, though, the poem's oppositions waver under close examination; but this poem is much more prepared to admit and discuss these uncertainties. The beggar inadvertently mimes the charity he is shown; and the way in which he does so comments disturbingly on the nature of charity itself.

> He sate, and eat his food in solitude;
> And ever, scatter'd from his palsied hand,
> That still attempting to prevent the waste,
> Was baffled still, the crumbs in little showers
> Fell on the ground, and the small mountain birds,
> Not venturing yet to peck their destin'd meal,
> Approached within the length of half his staff.

The numbness of the beggar's inner life is familiar from 'Old Man Travelling'—'never knowing that he sees...he is so still/ In look and motion'. But is the charity he receives not equally unconscious and involuntary? Its spontaneity is valued:

> ...the poorest poor
> Long for some moments in a weary life
> When they can know and feel that they have been
> Themselves the fathers and the dealers out
> Of some small blessings...

Elsewhere this sturdy individualism becomes less straightforward. Those who give to him also find themselves 'insensibly dispos'd/ To virtue and true goodness' which results when 'habit does the work/ Of reason'. In this language it is hard to claim credit for being understanding and generous. When the villagers' self-consciousness is aroused, it is in 'self-congratulation', resulting from a sense of difference rather than kinship with the old man, 'each recalling his peculiar boons,/ His charters and exemptions'. The community is 'baffled' into generosity in its turn by a man who 'appears/ To breathe and live but for himself alone'. It is his resistant, charity-provoking otherness around which the communal sense of belonging crystallises. The alternative is 'that vast solitude' in which the beggar lives: a vacuum in which individuality is free to expand almost beyond recognition. The poem argues that there is nothing *outside* the social definition of people just as there is nothing *inside* the old beggar, save 'the natural silence of old age'. That is why, in confronting him through charity, people recall instead their own social privilege and status. This only ceases to be a patronising or cynical attitude to the beggar when it is realised that his life, 'free of mountain solitude' and 'in the eye of nature', is an object of desire as much as a means of refusing or controlling that desire. An unencumbered existence beyond society, as if one could owe allegiance only to the universal human character which Wordsworth's poetry tries to grasp, a 'life and soul to every mode of being/Inseparably link'd', is tied to a cautionary tale of poverty, decrepitude and silence.

Love

The visionary expansion of the individual beyond social restraint to embody 'Nature's law' or 'one human heart' is both wished for and made unacceptable by poems like 'The Old Cumberland Beggar'. In Wordsworth's erotic poems, a neglected category, this politics of self-definition is investigated further. In 'Ruth', a woman is reduced to beggary and idiocy through a series of surrenders to nature, the crucial one of which is sexual. In 'Nutting', which originally opened with an address to 'Lucy', Wordsworth uses the boy's relationship with nature to question the will to force the two halves of his argument, radical and conservative, together. Erotic desire and love here enhance their object until it has unprecedented value, yet in order to live with it in an ordinary world. 'Nutting' tells the story of an erotic engagement with nature which turns into violation and destruction. The boy puts on a beggar's disguise so that thorns, brakes and brambles can do their worst: he can approach one of nature's secret places without discomfort or loss. As a beggar, he is also adopting the extra-social role we have seen Wordsworth use to characterise a free and natural existence. He reaches a bower, which could have been Ruth's, and contemplates its beauty for while. Then,

> ...up I rose,
> And dragg'd to earth both branch and bough, with crash
> And merciless ravage; and the shady nook
> Of hazels, and the green and mossy bower,
> Deform'd and sullied, patiently gave up
> Their quiet being: and unless I now
> Confound my present feelings with the past,
> Even then, when from the bower I turn'd away,
> Exulting, rich beyond the wealth of kings
> I felt a sense of pain when I beheld
> The silent trees and the intruding sky.

He ends up 'rich beyond the wealth of kings', yet disappointed. Within the social dynamics of his approach there is no room for genuinely reciprocal relationship. His enjoyment of nature is framed by a caricature of capitalist success—a tale of rags to riches. The 'quiet being' he has forced the bower to surrender is not something to be possessed on those terms, if at all. Rape and a succeeding *tristitia* are what are immediately evoked. But the impossibility of any real intercourse between the child and the bower leaves the language of violent sexual possession to stand, as it were, on its own feet; and down it falls.

Wordsworth's criticism cuts both ways. The child's desire for the bower—'voluptuous, fearless of a rival'—is the immature anticipation of sexual relationship within the human community. Yet the way in which he misguidedly closes with the bower reveals a violence inherent in the common language of sexual engagement, and is not just provoked by the incongruity of his feelings for the bower. The poem is richer, though, than its slightly comic critique of capitalist notions of relationship as ownership or possession. The child's immaturity could easily explain their use as well—these are as yet the only ideas he has of what might satisfy his desire. The narrator carefully distances himself from the child, sharing his misgivings, but not the triumphant feelings they replace. The poem ends inconclusively: 'there is a Spirit in the woods', a self in nature to which we can relate; but how or why is left unspecified. The poem asks questions too big for itself, as if it were an excerpt from a larger poem like *The Prelude*.

The 'Lucy' poems, on the other hand, describe a love which, just as it appears adequate and unselfish, has to relinquish its object. In 'Strange Fits of Passion' the strength of the narrator's love for Lucy is indicated by the way in which he thinks that all nature contributes to his personal drama. 'In one of those sweet dreams I slept,/ Kind Nature's gentlest boon'. His dream of love is imaged as a harmony with natural movements converging on Lucy's cottage. But he is rudely awakened.

> And, all the while, my eyes I kept
> On the descending moon.

My horse mov'd on; hoof after hoof
He rais'd and never stopp'd:
When down behind the cottage roof
At once the planet dropp'd.

What fond and wayward thoughts will slide
Into a Lover's head—
'O mercy!' to myself I cried,
'If Lucy should be dead!'

Nature, naturally going its own way, refuses to cooperate. The significance of the sinking moon can only be morbid. His love for Lucy leads him to surrender her in imagination to a process larger than herself, of which she may unexpectedly appear the victim. The poem mocks the conventional exaggerations of love-songs; but at the same time its final uncompromising transition suggests seriously that to love someone is to cherish them to such a degree that through them you identify your deepest anxieties and fears, as well as your hopes and desires. The poem then can risk a disturbing complicity between the narrator's love for Lucy and the thought of her death—that final, loving roundedness the thought lends her image.

This, at any rate, is also the experience of the narrator of the other 'Lucy' poems. In 'She dwelt among th'untrodden ways', the narrator especially feels Lucy's 'difference', her particularity, most strongly when she is dead. He describes her as if she were a thing, only to agonise over the implications of the perfect otherness this description has successfully evoked.

A Violet by a mossy stone
Half-hidden from the Eye!
—Fair, as a star when only one
Is shining in the sky!
She *liv'd* unknown, and few could know

71

When Lucy ceas'd to be;
But she is in her Grave, and Oh!
The difference to me.

Here 'difference' is the creator of value as well as
individuality, but through absence and not presence or
possession. The narrator's egotism is paradoxically self-
lacerating, because of its admission that he defines himself
vicariously in loving another person. The 'Lucy' poems
show what a dangerous activity this is, implying as it does a
surrender to the figurative imagination, its daring ventures
and painful retreats.

Similarly, in 'Michael', the old shepherd of that name
gives away his son before his land because, for him, the latter
imaginatively defines the former: 'these fields, these hills/
Which were his living Being, even more/ Than his own
Blood'. Patrimony precedes paternity. This noble increase in
personality, in which identity encompasses a whole locality,
contains the tragic fragilities which Wordsworth's poems
instruct us to look for. The son's character changes when he
goes to the city to earn enough money to keep the
'patrimonial fields' in the family. The only kind of human
relationships in the poem are like those the narrator initially
has with the shepherds—'men/ Whom I already lov'd, not
verily/ For their own sakes, but for the fields and hills/
Where was their occupation and abode'. To own land is to
'possess it, free as the wind/ That passes over it'. This is
another of those natural and liberated existences incapable of
social incorporation. Michael's son is predictably defenceless
against the city's blandishments. No further explanation of
his degeneracy is given: for a character as rooted in place,
migration must be fatal.

In the 'Poems on the Naming of Places', the focus narrows
to the relations between Wordsworth and the small like-
minded community of friends at Grasmere: the 'happy band'

of 'Home at Grasmere'—Dorothy, the Hutchinson sisters, Coleridge, and occasionally Wordsworth's brother, John. Characters here do not grow to tragic stature. The identification of someone with a natural scene is rather a way of exploring the quality of the narrator's attraction to that person. All that takes place is a naming. This can create allegory, as in the poem to Mary Hutchinson where Wordsworth's desire for marriage endeavours, at the same time, to keep Mary delicately distanced and untouched.

> The spot was made by Nature for herself:
> The travellers know it not, and 'twill remain
> Unknown to them; but it is beautiful,
> And if a man should plant his cottage near,
> Should sleep beneath the shelter of its trees,
> And blend its waters with his daily meal,
> He would so love it that in his death-hour
> Its image would survive among his thoughts. . .

The poem to Dorothy, 'It was an April Morning', is not emblematic in this way. As in 'There is an Eminence', the subject is not identified with the geography of a place, which could release sexual meanings beyond the narrator's control, but with the shared perception, the act of naming:

> I gaz'd and gaz'd, and to myself I said,
> 'Our thoughts at least are ours; and this wild nook,
> My EMMA, I will dedicate to thee'.

Dorothy is someone he has 'lov'd/ With such communion', as the parallels between her journals and many of his early poems prove. The effort to comprehend nature's arbitrary profusion immediately reminds him of her. The poem strives to mean no more than that. The revealing figures of desire with which nature supplies the imagination, and which Dorothy and William might embarrassingly share, are left unspecified. Naming tries to stop short of interpretation. The poem seeks to denote rather than perform a poetic act, otherwise it might become another love-poem. Dorothy remains discreetly unpersonified.

Even within the community of the Wordsworths and their friends love is only allowed to enhance the loved one in ways which are kept under strict control. As in the more public poems, the limitations are as much the subject-matter of the poetry as the increases in personality. Already Wordsworth had begun *The Prelude*, a poem in which a poet confronts directly the constraints on self-consciousness in his own case. His initial, conspicuously literary investigation is gradually broadened, as succeeding versions of the poem incorporate the wider social and political considerations rehearsed in many of *Lyrical Ballads*. It goes further, though, in focusing these within a single, historical individual, and making the problem of generalising from this particular case its presiding question. It maps the natural limits of the visionary conception of the individual as it was available in a period of post-revolutionary disillusionment: 'this time/ Of dereliction and dismay'. The aim is to justify the poetic vocation not only to the poet, but also to those for whom recent political 'experiments' had thrown into disrepute, 'with sneers/ On visionary minds', poetry or any imaginative exploration of the self.

Chapter Four

New Beginnings

Wordsworth and his sister Dorothy settled in Grasmere in December 1799. It was a time of new beginnings. Wordsworth had in all likelihood just finished writing the 'glad preamble'—the passage which was to form the opening of the 1805 *Prelude*. The piece of blank verse to be known as the Prospectus to *The Excursion* was probably begun almost immediately afterwards; and in the spring of 1800 Wordsworth was at work on the poem to which it originally provided a climactic coda—'Home at Grasmere'. This is another of those Wordsworthian efforts hidden from his public (it was finally published in 1888) and crucial for understanding the poems to come. It was intended as the first part of *The Recluse* or, as the Preface to *The Excursion* has it, 'meditations in the Author's own person' within 'a philosophical poem containing views of Man, Nature and Society'—the *magnum opus* which Wordsworth never finished. However the next long poem he wrote after 'Home at Grasmere' was the rest of *The Prelude*, and it is that poem, not *The Excursion* or 'intermediate part' of *The Recluse*, for which it prepares us.

'Home at Grasmere' shows Wordsworth's conception of the self growing to its most generous, as he clears the ground for a great biographical poem. It is the apotheosis of that strain of thought in which he seeks to engage with a wider reality from a position of domestic seclusion. At first it appears inconsistent, omitting to take decisions between the alternative descriptions of 'reality' offered by Grasmere. The narrator insists on the paradisical nature of the valley, this 'blissful Eden'. He tries to dispel any doubts that he and Emma, 'A pair seceding from the common world', have arrived anywhere other than 'A Centre...A whole without dependence or defect'. This is a 'self-sufficing world', 'hallowed', 'holy', 'perfect Contentment, Unity entire', one whose 'society' is 'true community'. This quality of relationship is at first personal: the love between the narrator and Emma discreetly evoked early on:

> Her Voice was like a hidden Bird that sang;
> The thought of her was like a flash of light
> Or an unseen companionship, a breath
> Or fragrance independent of the wind...
>   (110–13)

It soon grows to include the cottagers, 'untutored shepherds' and all the flora and fauna whose lives it subsequently describes in cyclical, repetitive analogies which show how 'solitude is not/ Where these things are' (807–8).

However, these confident descriptions exist side by side with a strain of millenarian imagery which implies that present satisfactions are incomplete and can only symbolise a fulfilment still to come. The sufficiency of Grasmere is stressed to counter accusations that it is the retreat of those escaping from the truth of 'these unhappy times' and 'dreaming of unruffled life'. Once this point is made, though, local beauties, such as Hart-leap Well, paradoxically become an 'intimation of the milder day/ Which is to come, the fairer world than this' (238–9). This symbolic vision can only be imaginatively sustained. Like Milton, Wordsworth moves from describing Paradise as a place, to finding that it exists as a state of mind—the most constructive response to nature imaginable. Paradise becomes a narrative rather than an immediate sensation, a myth rather than a presence: the serpent enters, 'the sting is added', man himself/ For ever busy to afflict himself' (842–3). Paradise is artificial: Wordsworth uses the word 'deceive' to describe the effect of Grasmere's power 'to bear us on/ Without desire in full complacency' (393–5). Grasmere is only the stop-gap of 'the insatiable mind' (848), and the poem's argument is now in some disarray. Earlier, 'the Realities of Life' which Wordsworth had abandoned for Grasmere are honestly described as being, in his case, far from harsh:

> Yes, the Realities of Life—so cold,
> So cowardly, so ready to betray,
> So stinted in the measure of their grace,
> As we report them, doing them much wrong—
> Have been to me more bountiful than hope,
> Less timid than desire.
>
> (54–9)

The trouble is that Grasmere's superiority, its alternative centrality, now consists in being a symbol of hope rather than a 'self-sufficing world'. It is no longer to be prized for its pastoral virtues; its beneficial influence is rather to educate Wordsworth's timid desires—timid precisely because they might rest content with pastoral pleasures.

> But 'tis not to enjoy, for this alone
> That we exist; no, something must be done.

77

> I must not walk in unreproved delight
> These narrow bounds and think of nothing more...
>
> (875–8)

The landscape, therefore, appears most vividly to him when it comes as the sign of something else. Wordsworth occasionally calls this transcendental signified 'God', as when he bows low in the 1799 *Prelude* 'To God who thus corrected my desires'; or feels in the 1805 version, with Hartley, that his soul 'passing through all Nature rests with God'. But these are isolated moments of certainty. 'Home at Grasmere' fails to become the first part of *The Recluse* because it returns to the argument of *The Prelude*, an argument which Wordsworth had not finished working out until 1805. *The Prelude* generally accepts that experience exists in a state of incompleteness, process, change and development: 'With faculties still growing, feeling still/ That whatsoever point they gain they still/ Have something to pursue' (II.369–71). It is founded on the paradox, for which the child's immaturity is the dominant symbol, that the depth of satisfaction to be gained from natural beauty depends on its power to evoke desire, or the state of not being satisfied: 'something evermore about to be' (6.542).

In 'Home at Grasmere' Wordsworth fails to write a pastoral idyll and reverts to the psychological perspectives of *The Prelude*, to which he had probably just called a temporary halt in its first, two-part form in 1799. The magnificent peroration at the end of 'Home at Grasmere'— 'On Man, on Nature, and on human Life,/Thinking in solitude'—later used as the Prospectus to *The Excursion*, proposes a similarly comprehensive portrait of 'the mind of Man/ My haunt and the main region of my song'. *The Prelude*'s paradox is played out here in terms of visionary and ordinary perception. Visionary superiority—a landscape of desire—asserts itself by trying to have its own imaginary categories accepted as natural, rather than revising, in Blakean fashion, our notions of the normal and ordinary.

> ...Paradise and groves
> Elysian, fortunate islands, fields like those of old
> In the deep ocean—wherefore should they be
> A History, or but a dream, when minds
> Once wedded to this outward frame of things
> In love, find these the growth of common day?
> (996–1001)

. Conversely, the perfection of the place is to make the visionary apply—to turn epistemology into a mystic marriage, to transform perception into an animated, loving reciprocity of mind and nature.

In this Prospectus Wordsworth daringly invokes a 'greater Muse' than Milton's:

> Jehovah, with his thunder, and the quire
> Of shouting angels and the empyreal throne—
> I pass them unalarmed. The darkest Pit
> Of the profoundest Hell, chaos, night,
> Nor aught of [blinder] vacancy scooped out
> By help of dreams can breed such fear and awe
> As fall upon us often when we look
> Into our minds, into the mind of Man,
> My haunt, and the main region of my song.
> (982–90)

To understand what is at issue here it is helpful to bring Blake's short but pithy critique of the Prospectus to bear on the discussion. Wordsworth's complementary balance of vision and nature, desire and reality, in which one enhances the other, raised Blake's suspicions; especially when Wordsworth went on to elaborate his idea in a mechanical metaphor:

> How exquisitely the individual Mind
> (And the progressive powers perhaps no less
> Of the whole species) to the external world
> Is fitted; and how exquisitely too—
> Theme this but little heard of among men—
> The external world is fitted to the mind;
> And the creation (by no lower name
> Can it be called) which they with blended might
> Accomplish: this is my great argument.
>
> (1006–14)

Blake rightly sensed a cramping, legislatory function in Wordsworth's mechanical metaphor: 'You shall not bring me down to believe such fitting & fitted, I know better & please your Lordship'. Blake thought that vision would always be the loser in the kind of exchange Wordsworth envisaged. Desire would always be assimilated to some unchallenged notion of what was natural, losing its revolutionary potential, its critical bite, forgetful of its exorbitant claims. And just in case it did become disruptive Wordsworth was always ready to postpone its satisfaction.

This is clear from the passage in the Prospectus which comes between the naturalising of vision as 'the growth of common day' and the 'fitted' metaphor:

> I, long before the blissful hour arrives,
> Would sing in solitude the spousal verse
> Of this great consummation, would proclaim—
> Speaking of nothing more than what we are—
> How exquisitely the individual Mind...
>
> (1002–6)

This millenarian escape-clause undermines in the Prospectus what has been undermined throughout 'Home at Grasmere': the emphasis on the fulfilments possible in the here and now. The Prospectus had tried to suggest that its humanism

improved on Milton's Christian hope; that it was too
realistic to be put off with ideal promises. In a related passage
in Book 10 of the 1805 *Prelude* Wordsworth describes the
practical optimism of liberals who, after the death of
Robespierre, felt that they

> Were called upon to exercise their skill
> Not in Utopia—subterraneous fields,
> Or some secreted island, heaven knows where—
> But in the very world which is the world
> Of all of us, the place in which, in the end,
> We find our happiness, or not at all.
>   (10.722-7)

Blake, had he read this, might have doubted the political
commitment behind its optimistic realism, sensing the
domestication of revolutionary ideals rather than a call
uncompromisingly to act them out. Milton was much more
radical politically than Wordsworth. Wordsworth's effort to
envision more than Milton does seems plausible when he
claims to be demystifying or humanising Milton's religious
vision by translating its paradisical topography into accessible experience—'the growth of common day'. But Milton
the regicide was willing to take the practical revolutionary
steps he thought necessary to establish God's rule on earth.
Wordsworth's competing concept of poetry always aspires
towards a comprehensive sensitivity to the Edenic possibilities in sheer perception which forestalls the need to
improve the things perceived.

The passage in the Prospectus from 'I long before...'
through the 'fitted' metaphor to 'this is my great argument'
does not occur in the earliest manuscript and may well have
been added in 1806. If this is so, its claim to be 'Speaking of
nothing more than what we are' summarises the discoveries
of the 13-part *Prelude* of 1805. The tension throughout the
Prospectus between being satisfied with describing 'the

growth of common day' and envisioning 'the image of a better time' *is*, for Wordsworth, 'nothing more than what we are'. His liberal hesitancy between alternatives is different from Milton's and Blake's revolutionary singlemindedness. Yet, once again, Wordsworth shows how poetry as an institution can stretch to accommodate contradictory sympathies and reservations which would disqualify each other in other forms of writing, but which define poetically for him a complete response to experience.

Towards the end of the Prospectus Wordsworth confidently invokes the 'Soul of Man' in its most generous conception—identified with nature and expressed in poetry:

> Thou human Soul of the wide earth that hast
> Thy metropolitan Temple in the hearts
> Of mighty Poets...
>
> (1027–9)

The 'metropolitan Temple' is another of those Wordsworthian figures for the institutional character of poetry, the society constructed by the range of its sympathies—the 'mansion for all lovely forms' of 'Tintern Abbey'; 'the household of man' of the Preface to *Lyrical Ballads*; 'that interminable building reared/ By observation of affinities' of the 1799 *Prelude*; or the ante-chapel...to the body of a gothic church', as he calls *The Prelude* in the Preface to *The Excursion*, in which his shorter poems furnish 'the little cells, oratories, and sepulchral recesses, ordinarily included those edifices'. It is the argument of the 1805 *Prelude* which justifies Wordsworth's professional confidence in his 'metropolitan Temple', explaining in detail the evolution of social sympathies out of isolated imaginative engagements with nature. 'Home at Grasmere', trying to secularise an inherited Miltonic millenarianism, does not yet establish the logic of this development in its own terms—a logic which can now be seen more clearly to be implicit in the question raised at the start of the two-part *Prelude* of 1799 and finally answered by the full-blown argument of 1805.

The Two-Part Prelude of 1799

Wordsworth initially thought of *The Prelude* as yet another unpublished apprentice poem. In the Preface to *The Excursion* of 1814, he described the subsidiary part *The Prelude* played in his ambitious plan for a philosophical poem.

> Several years ago, when the Author retired to his native Mountains, with the hope of being able to construct a literary Work that might live, it was a reasonable thing that he should take a review of his own Mind, and examine how far Nature and Education had qualified him for such employment. As subsidiary to this preparation, he undertook to record, in Verse, the origin and progress of his own powers, as far as he was acquainted with them. That Work, addressed to a dear Friend, most distinguished for his knowledge and genius, and to whom the Author's Intellect is deeply indebted, has been long finished; and the result of the investigation which gave rise to it was a determination to compose a philosophical Poem, containing views of Man, Nature, and Society; and to be entitled, The Recluse; as having for its principal subject the sensations and opinions of a Poet living in retirement.—The preparatory Poem is biographical, and conducts the history of the Author's mind to the point when he was emboldened to hope that his faculties were sufficiently matured for entering upon the arduous labour which he had proposed to himself. . .

Within the history of *The Prelude* alone, though, there is a further series of trial runs and incomplete states. There are three main versions of the poem. The first is the two-part

83

Prelude written during 1798–99 in Germany and England. Recently, this shorter version has been more highly thought of than the longer work of 1805 and the much revised and first published form of 1850. The 1799 *Prelude* is certainly more obviously unified in theme than the longer 13-and-14-book versions. However, the shorter, neater version's main ideas point to the need for expansion and explain Wordsworth's efforts to draw out its significance. The style of the poem—its unmistakeable, long, blank verse sentences full of qualification and subtly modified recapitulation—makes the reader immediately aware of the predominant effort to express processes of mental growth and change always suggestive of the need for further exposition.

Shelley and others were amused at the apparent limitations of Wordsworth's view of experience. They sensed a prudery in the published poems which provoked Shelley's laughter in his parody *Peter Bell III*.

> But from the first 'twas Peter's drift
> To be a kind of moral eunuch,
> He touched the hem of Nature's shift,
> Felt faint—and never dared uplift
> The closest, all-concealing tunic.

But the truth is rather that Wordsworth had invested nature with so much emotional content, and conceived of it as being so capable of relationship, that he found it easy to neglect the complexities of sexual feelings between people. His narrator's 'Slight shocks of young love-liking' (4.325), presumably for the 'Frank-hearted maids of rocky Cumberland' (6.13), must have been more important, more formative than the awkward asides suggest. In *Lyrical Ballads*, Wordsworth often implicates loved ones with the image of a vast receptiveness in order to articulate the gains and losses experienced in love for them. In *The Prelude*, women are idealised, like Mary of Buttermere, Vaudracour's

Julia, the autobiographical Mary Hutchinson and Dorothy, or else their shamelessness puts them beyond the pale. Nature alone takes on the responsibility for focusing desire, most convincingly when Wordsworth is dealing with childhood.

The childhood experiences which the 1799 *Prelude* gives in quick succession show that the landscape remembered by the narrator is a landscape of wants as explicit as those of 'Nutting'. The child's 'unconscious intercourse' with nature turns the dream-like oneness intermittently explored in *Lyrical Ballads* into a mixed tale of beauty and terror. Childish depredations and stealthy satisfactions conjure up stern figures of reproach. Reflective ecstasies and adventurous excursions reveal 'meanings of delight, of hope and fear' (I.197). The child traps woodcock, goes on perilous bird-nesting expeditions, suffers visionary admonishment for stealing a boat, and in his 'boyish sports' generally feels 'Impressed upon all forms the characters/ Of danger or desire' (I.194–5). In these 'spots of time', as they are called in *The Prelude*, the child enjoys an imaginative expansion so powerful, so educative, that it seems to him that he is in the charge of a superior power which makes his entire environment minister to his needs.

Part I of the 1799 *Prelude* describes a child's exploration of his self-defining fears and desires through his narcissistic enjoyment of nature. Although nature's sufficiency to him is stressed, with this comes not an evasion of social and sexual elements in the child's development. Rather, as in 'Nutting', Wordsworth captures their infantile quality by showing that they *can* be discussed entirely through the child's reactions to his natural environment. At that time, this was the form in which 'Strong desire/Resistless overpowered' (I.42–3). The child's adventure in the stolen boat, for example, his 'elfin pinnace' purloined with the assured authority of 'one who proudly rowed/ With his best skill', shows the fraught, apprehensive form in which adult passions are experienced by him at that time. The child cannot enjoy such freedoms without simultaneously imagining adult censorship of his presumption.

> She was an elfin pinnace; twenty times
> I dipped my oars into the silent lake,
> And as I rose upon the stroke my boat
> Went heaving through the water like a swan—
> When from behind that rocky steep, till then
> The bound of the horizon, a huge cliff,
> As if with voluntary power instinct,
> Upreared its head. I struck, and struck again,
> And, growing still in stature, the huge cliff
> Rose up between me and the stars, and still,
> With measured motion, like a living thing
> Strode after me. With trembling hands I turned,
> And through the silent water stole my way
> Back to the cavern of the willow-tree.
> There in her mooring place I left my bark,
> And through the meadows homeward went with grave
> And serious thoughts; and after I had seen
> That spectacle, for many days my brain
> Worked with a dim and undetermined sense
> Of unknown modes of being. In my thoughts
> There was a darkness—call it solitude,
> Or blank desertion—no familiar shapes
> Of hourly objects, images of trees,
> Of sea or sky, no colours of green fields,
> But huge and mighty forms that do not live
> Like living men moved slowly through my mind
> By day, and were the trouble of my dreams.
>
> (I.103–29)

The child's act is suggestive in a way which he could not understand or interpret. Equally, the rebuke which he imaginatively receives goes far beyond what an adult would think appropriate for taking a shepherd's boat without asking. Wordsworth manages to be true to the exaggerations of the child's guilt, and to reveal an imaginative process at work much more ambitious in its power of explanation.

Such childish hyperbole helps foreground *The Prelude*'s main theme. The child's later self often mourns as a 'falling off' from an initial, intense intimacy with nature something which reveals the extent to which he constructs his own experience. 'The props of my affections were removed,/ And yet the building stood, as if sustained/ By its own spirit'(ll.324-6). The apparently unfortunate loss of original stimulus is offset by an enlivened awareness of the creativity, 'the building', which has shaped natural enjoyment. Such nominal defeats are only stages on the road to the confident conclusion of the 1805 *Prelude*, establishing 'how the mind of man becomes/A thousand times more beautiful than the earth/On which he dwells' (13.446-8). The poetic descriptions of childhood, grouped together in the 1799 *Prelude*, begin the 'Hard task to analyse a soul' (ll.263). And it is largely through their perceptive mingling of imagination and desire that we see why the poem has to expand into the larger versions: why love of nature has to lead to love of mankind; how the individual's imaginative response to his surroundings raises questions about the way in which people typically construct experience; how the child's invention of an interested, responsive world anticipates adult creations of social and political reality, a world which answers *their* needs.

This conceptual leap is basic to the plot of the 13-part *Prelude* of 1805; but the impetus for the larger poem is generated in its precursor of 1799. Its plot, described at the end of Part I, sounds straightforward; but in its appeal to Coleridge for a sympathetic reading it becomes indecisive.

> Meanwhile my hope has been that I might fetch
> Reproaches from my former years, whose power

> May spur me on, in manhood now mature,
> To honourable toil. Yet should it be
> That this is but an impotent desire—
> That I by such inquiry am not taught
> To understand myself, nor thou to know
> With better knowledge how the heart was framed
> Of him thou lovest—need I dread from thee
> Harsh judgements if I am so loth to quit
> Those recollected hours that have the charm
> Of visionary things, and lovely forms
> And sweet sensations, that throw back our life
> And make our infancy a visible scene
> On which the sun is shining?
>
> (I.450–64)

The effort to 'understand myself' may go unrewarded and appear instead a pleasurable but unconstructive indulgence of memory. It is also embarrassed by an obvious problem: the degree to which the present narrator reads back into his childhood experiences meanings which were not there for the child: there is an as yet unexplained identification of different kinds of perception which allows the otherwise contrasting 'charm/ Of visionary things' to contribute to 'a visible scene'. In one earlier and richly overburdened simile, Wordsworth describes this process of creative interpretation:

> ...yet I have stood
> Even while my eye has moved o'er three long leagues
> Of shining water, gathering, as it seemed,
> Through the wide surface of that field of light
> New pleasure, like a bee among the flowers.
>
> (I.408–12)

The accurate likening of the sea to a field of light disappears as Wordsworth develops the simile's logic of desire and peoples the sea with pleasurable flowers disseminated by his bee-like faculty of imagination. The final idea of the bee among the flowers has no place in the original image of 'a visible scene' which the poetic figure set out to enhance. In Part II of the 1799 *Prelude* the narrator admits that

> ...so wide appears
> The vacancy between me and those days,
> Which yet have such self-presence in my heart
> That sometimes when I think of them I seem
> Two consciousnesses...
>
> (II.26–30)

But the productive relation between these 'two consciousnesses' may mean that he can only grasp one at a time. The poet is only able to write as he does because of his formative childhood experiences; but he only establishes his vocation as a poet through his power to re-invade these experiences and illuminate them with an articulate significance that was not there before. In other words, he is only a poet in so far as he can *now* see these childhood experiences as being formative and incomplete, valuable as signs of something else. Wordsworth's description of them as 'spots of time' containing a 'fructifying virtue' tries to cover this ambivalence. He substitutes 'renovating' for 'fructifying' in 1805 and 1850, thus being less than straightforward about the way in which the poet's consciousness has grown out of the child's into something different. The more explicit Wordsworth becomes in his attempts to show consistency, the less successful he sounds. In fact the poem is unified without having to call the child a poet or the poet a child, although the simplicity of that solution is tempting: 'who would not give,/ If so he might, to duty and to truth/ The eagerness of infantine desire?' And frequently the child's experiences are described as cadenced or musical, as though he already grasps them as aesthetic. But the true unity of the poem comes from its investigation of a drive towards significance common to child and adult.

By that I mean the way in which the child's most immediate experiences of nature, his most literal assurances of its importance, paradoxically take the form of experiencing things as signs, as though they stand for something else. Nature in *The Prelude* is felt most pressingly at moments when it seems to gesture towards another thing. As in 'Home at Grasmere', it is often most tellingly *there* when its significance seems to lie elsewhere.

In the 'Immortality Ode' our soul 'hath elsewhere had its setting'; in the 1799 *Prelude* 'elsewhere' is even less substantial.

> Hard task to analyse a soul, in which
> Not only general habits and desires,
> But each most obvious and particular thought—
> Not in a mystical and idle sense,
> But in words of reason deeply weighed—
> Hath no beginning.
>
> (II.263–8)

There are no origins of meaning, only the desire for them and the 'interminable building' (432) raised in their pursuit. Nature's further significance remains indeterminate: attempts to explain it collapse into more renderings of the intensity of the original scene. This circularity of explanation is most explicit in the example of a spot of time following the description of spots of time in general.

> . . .I left the spot,
> And reascending the bare slope I saw
> A naked pool that lay beneath the hills,
> The beacon on the summit, and more near
> A girl who bore a pitcher on her head
> And seemed with difficult steps to force her way
> Against the blowing wind. It was in truth
> An ordinary sight, but I should need

Colours and words that are unknown to man
To paint the visionary dreariness
Which, while I looked all round for my lost guide,
Did at that time invest the naked pool,
The beacon on the lonely eminence,
The woman and her garments vexed and tossed
By the strong wind.

(I.313–27)

The landscape cries out for an allegorical interpretation, a 'lost guide', yet refuses it at the same time, coming full-circle back to the simple, guideless catalogue of pool, beacon, woman and wind. Its ordinariness is its most awesome quality, to be grasped only through the failure to translate it into something else. Yet the almost desperate need to transform, to try to escape in 'Colours and words that are unknown to man', the sufficiency of visionary dreariness, is its essence. The fact that the 'ordinary sight' is not a sign, yet is experienced as a sign, that it is not a metaphor, figure or symbol but demands a response to it as though it were, shows most strikingly the imaginative effort which *The Prelude* claims to be inherent in all human apprehension.

Indeterminacy of meaning in the spots of time thus cleverly keeps the expression of childhood experience free of hindsight, while linking it to maturer efforts to create a significant environment. The child's unspecifically symbolic appreciation of nature leads to an interest in symbolic procedures in general. We have seen how Wordsworth's personal talk can express a poetic sense of self in excess of any conventional form of understanding. The spots of time similarly gain their power to evoke a desire for meaning, rather than a particular meaning, by failing to symbolise an explanatory set of facts. The obvious progression for the poem is to consider the orders of signification—social, political, religious, and so on—which *do* offer explanations, and which the child grows to inherit. *The Prelude* then reviews them in the light of the intimations of poetic power given in the child's formative encounters with nature. In the 1805 *Prelude*, institutions of all kinds—literary and aesthetic as well as social and political, books and the Alpine sublime as well as Cambridge, London and revolutionary France—are evaluated for their capacity to accommodate the 'obscure sense of possible sublimity' granted the child.

However, it would be misrepresenting *The Prelude* to claim it as an entirely objective view, a complete cross-section of the culture of Wordsworth's time. Its autobiographical framework makes it a 'prelude', and distinguishes it from the scrupulously philosophical treatment, the 'abstruser argument' (11.176) which Wordsworth claims is still to come in *The Recluse*. There he intends to humanise Milton's effort to justify the ways of God to men, justifying instead the ways of men to men. He will do this in the light of a poetic understanding of the self for which human institutions legislate. The generosity of that poetic appreciation is explored in *The Prelude*, and personal limitations and accidental circumstances are to be overridden by its great project:

> ...we should ill
> Attain our object if, from delicate fears
> Of breaking in upon the unity
> Of this my argument, I should omit
> To speak of such effects as cannot here
> Be regularly classed, yet tend no less
> To the same point, the growth of mental power
> And love of Nature's works.
>
> (I.251–8)

The more limited format of the 1799 *Prelude* proposes a self-contained creative paradox: Wordsworth's worries that he has not lived up to the poetic promise of his childhood in fact provide him with his poem. But the expanded *Prelude*, despite its wordiness and occasional *longeurs*, establishes much more clearly and successfully the profounder character of Wordsworthian paradox. Poetry's important power to conceive of human fulfilment is enhanced by the failure of other institutions to cater for it. Yet this poetic advantage can easily seem nothing more than evidence of impracticality: not only in a utopian way, but also in the Wordsworthian sense of the poetic enlargement of experience as a frightening liberation fraught with unacceptable moral and political irresponsibility, 'an idle dream'. In the larger autobiographical context of the 1805 *Prelude*, poetry has to assert its rights in competition with other explanations of human experience. Wordsworth's vindication of himself to Coleridge as a poet has also become a justification for poetry: 'that the history of a poet's mind/ Is labour not unworthy of regard:/ To thee the work shall justify itself' (13.408–10).

Chapter Five

The 1805 Prelude: The Shepherd and the Cave

Book 8, with its 'Retrospect' showing 'Love of Nature Leading to Love of Mankind', established the larger argument of the 1805 *Prelude*. The mediating figure is that of the shepherd. He is not merely a feature of the place, a local on whom the narrator's eye happens to rest when undetained by mountains, cataracts and lakes. Wordsworth admires the shepherd's sturdy self-reliance; but neither this, nor his traditionally pastoral roles attract him: his power to take on figurative significance becomes of most importance. The shepherd enjoys a natural freedom which makes him a symbol of the larger self to which the child's imagination aspires. He is like 'a power/ Or genius', 'a giant stalking through the fog', 'glorified', 'sublime', 'ennobled', 'an index of delight'. The child outdoes literary abstractions in his appreciation of a 'creature—spiritual almost/ As those of books, but more exalted far,/ Far more of an imaginative form' (8.417–19). Yet the shepherd, it is conceded, is also an ordinary sight, 'a man/ With the most common' (423–4). Doesn't Wordsworth take the childish exaggeration too

94

seriously? To concentrate on exalted impressions of someone who, it is admitted, suffers 'with the rest/ From vice and folly, wretchedness and fear' (425-6) seems wilfully to ignore an often sordid reality.

Wordsworth's defence against this obvious objection leads us into the heart of *The Prelude*.

> Call ye these appearances
> Which I beheld of shepherds in my youth,
> This sanctity of Nature given to man,
> A shadow, a delusion?—ye who are fed
> By the dead letter, not the spirit of things,
> Whose truth is not a motion or a shape
> Instinct with vital functions, but a block
> Or waxen image which yourselves have made,
> And ye adore. But blessed be the God
> Of Nature and of man that this was so,
> That men did at the first present themselves
> Before my untaught eyes thus purified,
> Removed, and at a distance that was fit.
>   (8.428-40)

As in 'Tintern Abbey', meaning here is by nature mobile, not fixed by reference to a single object. It is a mistake to regard a figurative or metaphorical understanding of things as a disqualification from truth. Wordsworth does not give us grounds for believing in an original, literal grasp of reality, which he disparagingly calls 'the dead letter, not the spirit of things'. In *The Prelude*, a thing takes on meaning as it draws out the imaginative resources of the percipient, and so quickens with metaphorical life. We frequently lay claim to a realistic view of something by saying that we know what it is 'like': Wordsworth knew what shepherds were like. Our realism raises a simile; a moving target rather than a single impression or 'waxen image'; not one frame of the moving picture, but many. The child's untaught perception of the shepherd has a truth of its own for the older man because of this belief that meaning cannot stay still. The possibly mystifying and unrealistic distance at which the child sees the shepherd is taken to stand for the figurative distance, created by the imagination, at which all concepts stand to their objects. Any decision, therefore, to dismiss the child's vision as unrealistic or mystifying cannot be taken on purely epistemological grounds: it is no more figurative than its more literal-minded competitors. The commonness which subverts the 'glorified' image of the shepherd is like the ordinariness of the spot of time. That was grasped only in the failure to transform it imaginatively, in a 'visionary dreariness', itself a figure of oxymoron.

This theory of meaning is oriented with some pointedness in relation to other philosophers. Most striking is the disagreement with Plato when, in Book 8, Plato's famous simile of the cave is turned on its head. In Book 7 of *The Republic*, Plato had likened the quest for truth to the dilemma of being bound in a dark cave, looking at the wall on which are thrown the shadows of puppets passing in front of a fire somewhere behind the spectators. Enlightenment is achieved by slipping one's bonds and then getting out of the cave into sunlight, perceiving the unreality of the shadows and the deception of the puppets on the way. By contrast, Wordsworth gives us a simile which takes us *into* the cave, and rejoices in our power to manufacture the illusions from which Plato wants us to escape. Plato moves through degrees of reality, from the likenesses of things to the things themselves and the sun responsible for them. Wordsworth extols the ability to make out of the likenesses a world more lively than the originals.

> As when a traveller hath from open day
> With torches passed into some vault of earth,
> The grotto of Antiparos, or the den

Of Yordas among Craven's mountain tracts,
He looks and sees the cavern spread and grow,
Widening itself on all sides, sees, or thinks
He sees, erelong, the roof above his head,
Which instantly unsettles and recedes—
Substance and shadow, light and darkness, all
Commingled, making up a canopy
Of shapes, and forms, and tendencies to shape,
That shift and vanish, change and interchange
Like spectres—ferment quiet and sublime,
Which, after a short space, works less and less
Till, every effort, every motion gone,
The scene before him lies in perfect view
Exposed, and lifeless as a written book.
But let him pause awhile and look again,
And a new quickening shall succeed, at first
Beginning timidly, then creeping fast
Through all which he beholds: the senseless mass,
In its projections, wrinkles, cavities,
Through all its surface, with all colours streaming,
Like a magician's airy pageant, parts,
Unites, embodying everywhere some pressure
Or image, recognised or new, some type
Or picture of the world—forests and lakes,
Ships, rivers, towers, the warrior clad in mail,
The prancing steed, the pilgrim with his staff,
The mitred bishop and the throned king—
A spectacle to which there is no end.

(8.711-41)

Once more the significance of a natural scene lies in its figurative possibilities, in the suggestion that it might be the sign for something else, at a visionary departure, once again, from what might be found in a 'written book'. But the something else, could we recover it, would equally fail to close on an original satisfaction, and would also be 'some type/ Or picture of the world', making its own contribution

97

to 'A spectacle to which there is no end'.

Throughout *The Prelude* similar transfigurations keep taking place. To produce the imaginative reality latent in his environment is not necessarily Wordsworth's escape from disagreeables into 'the forests of romance' (5.477), equally bookish in their own way: it may, indeed, be a disquieting experience. The belief that the more fully we grasp things the more figurative our apprehension of them becomes, opens up vertiginous possibilities. As has been seen, it does not install positive revolutionary alternatives to established modes of understanding human nature, but sharpens our awareness of what we need them for. The poetry shows that we draw the line where we do, not on epistemological grounds, but for pragmatic reasons. That is why its visionary explorations usually still possess an ulterior literariness (here a kind of stock medievalism) which takes threatening figurations out of competition with scientific or political discourses. Like the ceiling of the cave, our norms are revived for us in imagination while remaining basically unchanged. In *The Prelude*, the poetic construction of reality thus becomes the stimulus of Wordsworth's liberal cultural critique.

Education—Cambridge and Books

In Book 12 Wordsworth complains 'How little that to which alone we give/ The name of education hath to do/ With real feeling and just sense' (12.168–72). He devotes the whole of Book 3 and some of Book 6 to discussing his experience of higher education at Cambridge. He went there after an upbringing which seemed in retrospect like having been 'trained up in paradise' (3.377). The endowments he brings to the university are described as being of a kind for which it cannot cater:

I was a freeman, in the purest sense
Was free, and to majestic ends was strong—
I do not speak of learning, moral truth,
Or understanding— 'twas enough for me
To know that I was otherwise endowed.

(3.89-93)

He is disillusioned with education for two reasons: it was out of touch with 'real feeling and just sense', and it was irrelevant to what he wanted to do.

Wordsworth happily criticises the narrowness of the curriculum, the enforcement of chapel attendance, the ignoble passions fostered by competitions for academic awards, and the quirkiness and intellectual frivolity of some of his aged teachers:

...grave elders, men unscoured, grotesque
In character, tricked out like aged trees
Which through the lapse of their infirmity
Give ready place to any random seed
That chooses to be reared upon their trunks.

(3.574-8)

They compare badly with the 'shepherd swains whom I had lately left', examples held up by 'Nature...in her great school' (580-6). But the criticism, however witty, is unhelpful because Wordsworth has not established a connection between the two schools of education, academic and natural. Cambridge is found wanting by both sets of standards, but Wordsworth still has to show how one set can be legitimately criticised by the other. How could academia develop a potential fostered by nature? All we are given is a sense of pure dissociation. Feelings of being at odds with Cambridge come out as a Christ-like sense of election: 'A feeling that I was not for that hour/ Nor for that place' (80-1).

Wordsworth leaves Cambridge, unable to combine the two schools of education. In Book 6 he states that only a concern for avoiding distress to his family stopped him from 'planning for myself/ A course of independent study' (6.38–9)—in other words, dropping out. His sense of election is only bolstered by Cambridge when, as in London, he conjures up the imaginary presence of 'generations of illustrious men'—Renaissance scholars, Spenser, Milton, Newton—who had studied there before him. But these sympathies are only the temporary, bookish cover for Wordsworth's deeper concern over how to express what he feels brought up to express. He cannot fit his childhood intimations, his sense of election, to the concept of knowledge offered to him by educational institutions. Yet he thinks the two ought to mesh, and feels his life suspended unproductively between them:

> ... my life became
> A floating island, an amphibious thing,
> Unsound, of spungy texture, yet withal
> Not wanting a fair face of water-weeds
> And pleasant flowers. The thirst of living praise,
> A reverence for the glorious dead, the sight
> Of those long vistos, catacombs in which
> Perennial minds lie visibly entombed,
> Have often stirred the heart of youth, and bred
> A fervent love of rigorous discipline.
> Alas, such high commotion touched not me...
> (3.339–49)

The amphibiousness of his life, wearing its natural cultivation on its 'face', alternates between this pretty surface and absorption in an indeterminate sub-aqueousness. The subsequent 'thirst', which might have imbued the 'spungy' function of his life with intelligence, is linked to a different order of underworld, subterranean this time, which does not fit into the original metaphor. This is reinforced by the fact that the desired 'commotion' could only have the pedagogical meaning required here (not of tumult, but of intellectual stirrings in emulation of 'the glorious dead' and 'Perennial minds') if we revive its 'dead' Latin etymology, suggesting a shared movement. The poetic control with which the passage evokes, through its subtly mismatched metaphors, the discontinuities in the student's education expresses 'commotion' in its opposite, unlearned sense; but it does so in a way which must emphasise a superior poetic learning, in command of both meanings of the word at once, genuinely amphibious.

Cambridge helps Wordsworth the poet not at all, except as it impresses upon him that poetry must itself take on responsibility for expressing the liberal education which he thinks academic institutions exclude. Sometimes the 'godlike hours' and 'majestic sway we have/ As natural beings in the strength of Nature' seem to Wordsworth 'far hidden from the reach of words' (3.193-4,185). However, he is more adept than most at showing how words can profit poetically from their literal failure. His subsequent review of various uses of words, especially books, develops his criticism of Cambridge, this time playing literary rather than educational institutions against his own sense of poetic election.

The 'Conclusion' to *The Prelude* concedes that 'much hath been omitted, as need was—/ Of books how much!' (13.279-80). The existing discussion of books in the poem is a revealing mixture of praise and blame. Wordsworth's originality as a poet sets him against his literary inheritance. In Book 12 he looks to Coleridge for praise at having caught 'a tone,/ An image, and a character, by books/ Not hitherto reflected' (12.363-5). This is not only a desire to be thought new. It follows soon after a passage in which Wordsworth attacks his own literary tradition in terms recalling the

Advertisement and Prefaces to *Lyrical Ballads*.

> Yes, in those wanderings deeply did I feel
> How we mislead eath other, above all
> How books mislead us—looking for their fame
> To judgements of the wealthy few, who see
> By artificial lights—how they debase
> The many for the pleasure of those few,
> Effeminately level down the truth
> To certain notions for the sake
> Of being understood at once, or else
> Through want of better knowledge in the men
> Who frame them, flattering thus our self-conceit
> With pictures that ambitiously set forth
> The differences, the outside marks by which
> Society has parted man from man,
> Neglectful of his universal heart.
>
> (12.205–19)

Wordsworth slanders a feminine readership in a liberal cause, making its books stand for a simple-minded cultural exclusiveness which perpetuates social division in the interests of 'the wealthy few'. But a few lines later, he finds that his 'theme/ No other than the very heart of man' is informed 'by books (good books, though few),/ In Nature's presence' (239–40, 243–4). The 'few' have changed from the socially and economically privileged into a Miltonic remnant, catching the rhythm of Milton's 'fit audience though few' of *Paradise Lost*. Books which can stand in 'Nature's presence' remain alive to that element in people which escapes or is larger than what they may have to say for themselves. Wordsworth goes on to describe characters for whom 'Words are but under-agents in their souls—/ When they are grasping with their greatest strength/ They do not breathe among them' (272–4). It is hard not to hear 'gasping' in 'grasping', an echo emphasising the continuity with 'breathe'. This would recall the Wordsworthian irony of using words to communicate powerfully through their difficulties. As was seen in *Lyrical Ballads*, words can be used poetically to convey this 'strength' in those who, because they are inarticulate, are 'unregarded by the world' (277).

The 'privilege' for which Wordsworth hopes is that a work of his 'Proceeding from the depth of untaught things,/ Enduring and creative, might become/ A power like one of Nature's' (310–12). In context, the 'untaught' can therefore mean those things overlooked for political reasons and only grasped creatively through an increase in sympathy. In Book 5 he praises books, from the 'loftiest notes' of Homer and the Old Testament down to 'ballad tunes'. Nevertheless, he criticises an education confined to books. He worries about books' physical frailty, yet he describes their strength as 'only less/ For what we may become, and what we need,/ Than Nature's self which is the breath of God' (5.220–2). Presumably a life restricted to books would, for Wordsworth, be a contradiction; for books, if appreciated fully, are open-ended in their power to suggest 'what we may become'. They do this, as Wordsworth thinks nature does, by showing us an apparently unstinted version of ourselves, grasped only in imagining it. But it also seems true that the more successful the book and the more engrossing its vision, the less we feel impelled to look outside it. The more their powers are 'like one of Nature's', the more books are likely to prove a false substitute for nature. In Book 5 Wordsworth blesses the 'dreamers.../ Forgers of lawless tales' because they 'make our wish our power, our thought a deed,/ An empire, a possession' (547–53). But if this wish-fulfilment is taken for sufficient reality, then, as in 'Nutting', it usurps the right of something else.

Certainly this usurpation will produce an exhilarating sense of our own powers. Books, like nature, can magnify the self which makes their world its own playground. But to entrust our sense of identity to so imaginary a category is

103

perilous—not simply from mistaking art for life, but from being committed to a view of life transfigured so as to satisfy all imaginative need. The analogical relation in which books stand to nature, the 'as if' or 'like', denotes an inferiority which Wordsworth is keen to preserve. By this means he can control his mobile, figurative realism, which elsewhere threatens to outrun all boundaries, with a literary catch-all. In comparison with nature's power to survive all changes, the frailty of books, which is lamented so feelingly at the start of Book 5, also teaches the folly of a life lived entirely on the same plane of existence as them. Hence his subsequent, and otherwise unconnected, cautionary tales of two characters who live in this way, the Arab and the 'dwarf man'.

Perhaps the most enigmatic passage in *The Prelude* is Wordsworth's story of the Arab who appears in a friend's dream, mounted on a dromedary, bearing a stone and a shell which are, he tells the friend, two books—*Euclid's Elements* and 'something of more worth'. The friend puts his ear to the shell and hears 'An ode in passion uttered, which foretold/ Destruction to the children of the earth/ By deluge now at hand' (97-9). The Arab lives as though the poetry spoken by the shell were true, burying the two books to save them from the flood which it foretells. To this kind of audience, poetry speaks so persuasively of its own frailty that it must be buried and listened to no more. Equally, one could say that its authority, its power to command assent, paradoxically necessitates its immediate preservation from a world it has shown to be about to flood, to lose its existing boundaries, becoming 'A spectacle to which there is no end', and disappear. Just before he dreamt of the Arab, the friend had been reading *Don Quixote*, one of the most famous warnings against the follies of a visionary life; and he dreams that the Arab is also 'the very knight/ Whose tale Cervantes tells' 123-4). Like a holy fool, the 'semi-Quixote' Arab attracts a sort of reverence for his errand; but that kind of total commitment to poetry's visionary power, its potentially apocalyptic message, also appears as the 'maniac's anxiousness': something which supplants familial and sexual ties to 'whatsoever else the heart holds dear; another 'idle dream' from which the friend must awake.

The 'dwarf man' is a child educated entirely by books. His precociousness especially repels the narrator. He has virtues: 'Briefly, the moral part/ Is perfect, and in learning and in books/ He is a prodigy' (5.318-20). But to have matured so early, to be 'The noontide shadow of a man complete' (297), with its accompanying vanities and self-love, has its drawbacks. This bookish world, because cut off from nature (rather than turning nature into the Arab's overwhelming tale), can lead nowhere. Wordsworth contrasts a child whose literary fantasies—'Jack the Giant-killer, Robin Hood' (366)—are in fact more serious than the 'dwarf man's' erudition because in them the child 'forgets himself', although under controlled, literary conditions. This links him without danger to 'the unreasoning progress of the world' (384)—a spontaneous growth of the self set free within ameliorating circumstances, not a tidal wave. The next educational example, the boy of Winander, has already been discussed in its excerpted form in *Lyrical Ballads*. He is one of 'A race of real children' (436) but becomes another casualty of visionary surrender. An education completely entrusted to an imaginative exchange with nature appears as dangerous as one confined to books. Wordsworth only presents a just balance between books and nature in the final tale told in Book 5.

This is the episode of the drowned man. The original of the incident was, appropriately, a local schoolmaster who drowned in Esthwaite Water when Wordsworth was nine years old. By a grisly irony, it is the man's death which is used to illustrate the educational value of books. The boy

watches a pile of abandoned clothes on the opposite shore of
the lake as evening falls.

> The succeeding day—
> Those unclaimed garments telling a plain tale—
> Went there a company, and in their boat
> Sounded with grappling-irons and long poles:
> At length, the dead man, 'mid that beauteous scene
> Of trees and hills and water, bolt upright
> Rose with his ghastly face, a spectre shape—
> Of terror even. And yet no vulgar fear,
> Young as I was, a child not nine years old,
> Possessed me, for my inner eye had seen
> Such sights before among the shining streams
> Of fairyland, the forests of romance—
> Thence came a spirit hallowing what I saw
> With decoration and ideal grace,
> A dignity, a smoothness, like the words
> Of Grecian art and purest poesy.
>
> (5.466–81)

In the 1799 *Prelude* this incident is yet another spot of time,
but lacking the explanation of the child's lack of fear,
concerned instead to show the fructifying virtue of the scene

> ...that impressed my mind
> With images to which in following years
> Far other feelings were attached—with forms
> That yet exist with independent life,
> And, like their archetypes, know no decay.
>
> (I.283–7)

This anticipates the logic of Wordsworth's anti-Platonic
simile of the cave. In 1805, with the main passage transposed
to the discussion of books, the habit of indulging such
imaginative departures steadies the child, who might
otherwise have been disabled by fright in the face of

shocking new experiences like the unimaginative Peter Bell seeing his 'dead man in the river'. The child is able to look more closely, to see more (as perhaps the traveller does by using his imagination in the cave), because he can draw aesthetic parallels, because he can see what it is 'like'. Wordsworth seems to have picked the incident carefully to illustrate this thesis. The 'decoration and ideal grace', the 'dignity', 'smoothness' and generally statuesque quality of the prototype in 'Grecian art and purest poesy' must have been literally true to the rigid, marmoreal form of the surfacing corpse. More of its genuine aspect is caught in the 'fairyland' comparison in which the 'ghastly' and the 'spectral' are the visual norm. What is still disturbing, as with the tale of the Arab, is the way it takes a drowning to elicit the realistic application: poetry can only conjure up a world outside books at the cost of its subject's identity.

Wordsworth concludes Book 5 with the birth of his delight in poetry: 'My ears began to open to the charm/ Of words in tuneful order, found them sweet/ For *their own sakes*—a passion and a power' (577-9). Poetry epitomises the educational logic which Wordsworth has been trying to demonstrate. In valuing words for their own sakes, one is already, in reading and pronouncing them, discovering patterns and images other than those in the objects to which they refer, those supposedly essential to their descriptive function. But this instinctive movement beyond immediate meaning to a figurative distance, brings poetry nearer to matching the infinite, endless, eternal 'motion' of nature. The end of Book 5 contains *The Prelude*'s most explicit identification of the two impulses.

> Visionary power
> Attends upon the motion of the winds
> Embodied in the mystery of words;
> There darkness makes abode, and all the host

> Of shadowy things do work their changes there
> As in a mansion like their proper home.
>
> (619–24)

The 'mystery' of words retains the older meaning of craft or profession, as well as the modern sense of obscurity or 'darkness'. In poetic appreciation, the imaginative shift to considering the words for their own sake seems to diminish the importance of denoting things. But it does so by capturing the 'wish for something loftier, more adorned' (599) in which Wordsworth believes human apprehension to be tutored by nature's power to outdistance all our expectations. The last passage quoted continues:

> Even forms and substances are circumfused
> By that transparent veil with light divine,
> And through the turnings intricate of verse
> Present themselves as objects recognised
> In flashes, and with a glory scarce their own.
>
> (625–9)

The figurative departures of poetry, 'the turnings intricate of verse', which can appear purely subjective, are accurate responses to something real. Poetry is not, for Wordsworth, only the expression of human imagination, but also the way in which 'forms and substances' can 'present themselves as objects'. The figurative mode of recognising them ('In flashes, and with a glory scarce their own') argues poetry to be the proper description of nature's power to expose as a metaphor or partial likeness anything posing as a finished definition.

London

London disappoints Wordsworth by parodying the natural greatness with which his imagination sympathises elsewhere.

The boy thinks of London as a fairy place, but this time his
bookish anticipations do not enhance a realistic understanding, but are merely inaccurate. London also has an infinite,
endless quality, but again this is a travesty of the way in
which nature draws out the percipient's imaginative resources at other times:

> ...the Babel din,
> The endless stream of men and moving things,
> From hour to hour the illimitable walk
> Still among streets...
>
> (7.157–60)

In Book 7, words like 'blank', 'moving', 'endless' and
'undistinguishable' lose their earlier portentousness and
indicate only the 'unmanageable sight' which London
presents to Wordsworth. The Lakeland tale of an abandoned
woman and child, Mary of Buttermere, typical lyrical ballad
material, is put on stage in London as a melodrama, the
erring husband 'a bold bad man' and the whole presentation
a cliché. But even Wordsworth's own touchstones of human
value become curiously artificial. The beautiful child he sees
being fêted among 'dissolute men/ And shameless women'

> ...hath since
> Appeared to me ofttimes as if embalmed
> By Nature—through some special privilege
> Stopped at the growth he had...
>
> (399–402)

Childhood here is not valued for its formative power,
dynamic and unsettling, but as a sentimental and implausibly
arrested state of innocence. Similarly, the first time he hears
'a woman utter blasphemy' and sees prostitutes, Wordsworth's sympathies are suddenly baffled, and the women
become unreal to him: 'a barrier seemed at once/ Thrown

in, that from humanity divorced/ The human form'
(7.424-6).

Book 7 is partly a controlled rendering of the frightened
sensibilities of a young provincial. But London in general
confronted him with an experience which successfully
resisted his imaginative sympathies. He shows more 'charitable pleasure' (466) in the theatre than in the street. His
galloping poetic participation in Bartholomew Fair, its
prodigies, freaks, side-shows, music, booths and crowds
finally draws back appalled by the fact that such sheer
histrionic display of 'trivial objects, melted and reduced/ To
one identity by differences/That have no law, no meaning,
and no end' (703-5) can actually describe human life. The
Arab's dream appears to have come true. But the Fair
proclaims a rival aesthetic in which what people have in
common is their idiosyncratic differences from each other.
The natural direction of Wordsworth's uncomic imagination, unlike Ben Jonson's in his play *Bartholomew Fair*, takes
exactly the opposite path.

> In spite of difference of soil and climate, of language and
> manners, of laws and customs, in spite of things silently gone
> out of mind and things violently destroyed, the Poet binds
> together by passion and knowledge the vast empire of human
> society...

As a 'pageant' or theatrical 'spectacle', Bartholomew Fair
asks the looker-on to enjoy the peculiarities which Wordsworth's sympathies, here described in the Preface to *Lyrical
Ballads*, try to overcome. For Wordsworth, parody and
burlesque are all right on the stage; but how to accept them
as one's form of existence defeats him entirely.

> All moveables of wonder from all parts
> Are here, albinos, painted Indians, dwarfs,
> The horse of knowledge, and the learned pig,

110

The stone-eater, the man that swallows fire,
Giants, ventriloquists, the invisible girl,
The bust that speaks and moves its goggling eyes,
The waxwork, clockwork, all the marvellous craft
Of modern Merlins, wild beasts, puppet-shows,
All out-o'-th'-way, far-fetched, perverted things,
All freaks of Nature, all Promethean thoughts
Of man—his dulness, madness, and their feats,
All jumbled up together to make up
This parliament of monsters.

(680–95)

These individual aberrations epitomise for him London's
senseless parody of a community, a 'parliament' whose
representativeness should make a nonsense of the very
notion of representation—'O, blank confusion, and a type
not false/ Of what the mighty is itself' (696–7).

All Wordsworth can do is once more to make a virtue out
of his feeling of dissociation. As in the famous sonnet
'Composed Upon Westminster Bridge', he is happiest when
the city is emptied of its turbulent populace. Then he is
struck by 'The calmness, beauty, of the spectacle,/ Sky,
stillness, moonshine, empty streets, and sounds/ Unfre-
quent as in deserts' (634–6). Or else he finds in the
anonymity of crowds the mysterious, simile-generating
profusion of nature:

How often in the overflowing streets
Have I gone forwards with the crowd, and said
Unto myself, 'The face of everyone
That passes by me is a mystery.'
Thus have I looked, nor ceased to look, oppressed
By thoughts of what, and whither, when and how,
Until the shapes before my eyes became
A second-sight procession, such as glides
Over still mountains, or appears in dreams...

(595–603)

111

He empties the people he meets of their individuality, their 'what, and whither, when and how', in the interests of cultivating a vision like that in the cave. It is 'in such mood' that he encounters the 'blind beggar', a figure apparently emptied in advance of any character which might pre-empt poetic response.

> Amid the moving pageant, 'twas my chance
> Abruptly to be smitten with the view
> Of a blind beggar, who, with upright face,
> Stood propped against a wall, upon his chest
> Wearing a written paper, to explain
> The story of the man, and who he was.
> My mind did at this spectacle turn round
> As with the might of waters, and it seemed
> To me that in this label was a type
> Or emblem of the utmost that we know
> Both of ourselves and of the universe,
> And on the shape of this unmoving man,
> His fixèd face and sightless eyes, I looked,
> As if admonished from another world.
>
> (610–23)

In this most complex description, the narrator's imagination raises another spectre of the flood. Confronting the vacant gaze of the blind beggar, his mind 'turns round/ As with the might of waters', sensing a visionary space in which the man's significance can expand immeasurably beyond the label pinned to his chest. His story, what the label says, remains untold, drowned in the story of the poetic response to it as 'type/ Or emblem of the utmost that we know'. However, this act of poetic rescue obscures the extent to which the beggar already was a creature of the written word, participating in the rival artistry of the 'moving pageant'. His immobility is used to suggest, implausibly, that he is doing something different from those around him. The fact that the label describes 'who he was' as well as his 'story' vanishes as he becomes like the citizen of another world with power to admonish this one. If we read the passage against the flow, opposing the almost irresistible tide of the narrator's self-expression, the vacant beggar remains nothing more than the story pinned on his chest, and the economic and material significance of *that* kind of impoverishment is acknowledged. But to do that allows him to share the same kind of theatrical existence as the other London exhibits who particularly distressed Wordsworth in Bartholomew Fair, similarly advertised in the 'staring pictures and huge scrolls,/Dumb proclamations of the prodigies' (666-7) by which they solicit custom. Yet this, presumably, is how the beggar lives? The poetry works up a contradiction in which the label on the beggar's chest allows him to be transported into a poetic realm of 'emblem' and 'story' in which he already exists by reason of his need to beg.

Wordsworth's critique of London in Book 7 sometimes amounts to little more than extolling a natural education obviously unavailable within the city. But the idea that corrupt city life already has its own poetic topography is a threatening one, denying Wordsworth's poetry both its critical authority and its visionary detachment. In Book 8, he is defensively dismissive of first reactions which might have given the impression of being 'ignorant that high things/ Were round me' (8.688-9). London, 'preceptress stern, that did instruct me next' (678), now has a recognised educational force of her own, a power to draw out that figurative capacity of the mind which at first she disruptively parodied. He tries to bind the monumental significance he now attributes to London to the life he sees within it: 'a sense/ Of what had been here done, and suffered here/ Through ages, and was doing, suffering, still' (782-4). The personal adventure of imagining an otherworldly reproach in the eyes of a blind beggar is replaced by the mute drama of the artificer and his sick child. The critique of London is condensed to the simpler, biting contradiction of a man who feels forced to protect his child from the life with which he wants to restore it.

> He held the child, and, bending over it
> As if he were afraid both of the sun
> And of the air which he had come to seek,
> He eyed it with unutterable love.
>
> (856–9)

Usurpations: The Alps and The French Revolution

When London is admired as a monument which educates the narrator in the sense that he 'Was not a punctual presence, but a spirit/ Living in time and space', its pedagogic function is like that of nature and books. It is described as part of the 'external universe' which 'By striking upon what is found within,/ Had given me this conception, with the help/ Of books and what they picture and record' (8.763–9). But London is deplored as a society which can only parody true community, although it is only with difficulty that its self-dramatisations are denied poetic authenticity. The most striking thing about the Alps described in Book 6 is also their power to disappoint. The key examples are the first sight of Mont Blanc, and the moment when Wordsworth and his companion realise that they have crossed the Alps. The former experience is of a natural image which, as London did initially, puts an end to imaginative speculation.

> That day we first
> Beheld the summit of Mount Blanc, and grieved
> To have a soulless image on the eye

Which had usurped upon a living thought
That never more could be.

(6.452–6)

Perhaps there is an implied critique of a sensation-seeking attitude towards nature: the growing cult of the 'sublime' which looked to nature for a thrilling astonishment unconnected with the educational process which Wordsworth is always at pains to demonstrate. The disappointment is quickly forgotten when the travellers catch sight of the glaciers at Chamonix, which made 'rich amends/ And reconciled us to realities' (460–1).

'Mount Blanc' appears to be an unimportant setback, but only until the tale of the discovery that there is no more climbing to come in the journey across the Alps. The narrator had mistakenly continued up a mountainside until a peasant informed him that his path led downwards from now on. The effect is exactly the opposite to that of seeing 'Mount Blanc'. This time, his imagination is not to be disappointed: its own quickening apprehension is not killed off by the natural image to lament what 'never more could be'. Instead, it is thrown into one of the most assured and direct celebrations of its authority in *The Prelude*. Imagination does the usurping now, foiling the finished outline of the Alps with its apprehension of 'something evermore about to be'.

Imagination!—lifting up itself
Before the eye and progress of my song
Like an unfathered vapour, here that power,
In all the might of its endowments, came
Athwart me. I was lost as in a cloud,
Halted without a struggle to break through,
And now, recovering, to my soul I say
'I recognize thy glory'. In such strength
Of usurpation, in such visitings

115

> Of awful promise, when the light of sense
> Goes out in flashes that have shown to us
> The invisible world, doth greatness make abode,
> There harbours whether we be young or old.
> Our destiny, our nature, and our home,
> Is with infinitude—and only there;
> With hope it is, hope that can never die,
> Effort and expectation, and desire,
> And something evermore about to be.
>
> (6.525–42)

Here, the halt in the poem's visible 'progress' towards an adequate image of imagination is transformed into a triumphant poetic progression. The new advance re-aligns apparent obstacles: it thrives on opposition ('Athwart me'), on obscurity ('lost as in a crowd'), even on extinction ('when the light of sense/ Goes out in flashes')—all generated by the simile of the imagination: 'Like an unfathered vapour' in which the poet recognises his own soul glorified. The startling 'unfathered' frees identity from the conventional patriarchal wisdom about origins like parenthood, just as the obstacle-words had been released from their ordinary connotations. This freedom or 'strength/ Of usurpation' leaves the poet unable to get his bearings other than through taking their absence to be directing him somewhere else in 'hope...Effort and expectation, and desire'. As in 'Tintern Abbey', the 'invisible world' is not described with metaphysical assurance, but is evoked in the poetic power of language to go on talking us through the uncertainties of an experience which has abandoned any such referential guarantees of meaning.

Wordsworth immediately insists that he has not been describing a power-struggle between mind and nature, imagination and the Alps, sense and reference; yet his imagery confesses to the battle which it claims did not take place.

The mind beneath such banners militant
Thinks not of spoils or trophies, nor of aught
That may attest its prowess, blest in thoughts
That are their own perfection and reward...
(543–6)

In fact, in his scheme, there can be no contest. His simile of
the cave was originally inserted between the bathos of 'We
had crossed the Alps' and the lines in celebration of the
resulting access of imaginative power. The simile would have
explained what happens next, which is the return to
prominence of nature after its failure to mark the summit of
the Alps with some suitably tremendous landmark. Nature
only impresses and regains favour once more by generating
for the mind another 'spectacle to which there is no end'.

The unfettered clouds and region of the heavens,
Tumult and peace, the darkness and the light,
Were all like workings of one mind, the features
Of the same face, blossoms upon one tree,
Characters of the great apocalypse,
The types and symbols of eternity,
Of first, and last, and midst, and without end.
(566–72)

The breathless transitions dramatise imagination's efforts to
embrace both sides in the mind–nature dispute by making
sense of them as 'blossoms upon one tree'. The closely
packed antitheses show rather than state the unbroken
growth of one out of the other: the conflicting 'workings of
one mind' ('Tumult and peace, the darkness and the light')
reveal a 'face' coming to expression in the inexhaustible
works of nature. The temptation to read into this face a
significance beyond nature is to some extent defused by the
syntactic parallel of apocalyptic 'Characters' with the
'eternity' belonging to nature and modelled throughout the

117

poem by its restless language of figurative departures or provocatively unsatisfying ordinariness. Mind and nature cannot do battle if nature can only strike home in imagined characters or poetic progressions which show it to advantage, surpassing attempts to fix it in literal truth. So why should precautions be taken against the interpretation of this mutually supportive relationship or dialectic as a series of insurrections?

The immediate answer is that usurpations were going on all around *The Prelude*'s travellers during their trip to France and the Alps. Wordsworth cannot have failed to discern the kinship between the autobiographical descriptions of his narrator's own imaginative education and the picture emerging of France's revolutionary re-evaluation of its society. When Wordsworth arrived in France on his first visit, an entire country seemed to embody the potential ascribed in *The Prelude* to his own upbringing. The famous lines, 'Bliss was it in that dawn to be alive,/ But to be young was very heaven!' (10.692–3), assimilate political change in France to the process of growth *The Prelude* has been tracing. Important words from the vocabulary of Wordsworth's development—'hope', 'freedom', 'prospect', 'promise', 'desire'—cluster now around public events. The narrator's description of his initial revolutionary partisanship could equally apply to a childhood foray in all its 'fructifying virtue'.

> Not caring if the wind did now and then
> Blow keen upon an eminence that gave
> Prospect so large into futurity—
> In brief, a child of Nature, as at first,
> Diffusing only those affections wider
> That from the cradle had grown up with me...
> (10.749–54)

This identification seemed simplistic to the older poet.

The younger man, feeling his poetic afflatus at one with radical enthusiasm, was inclined to excuse excesses or remain blind to the coming violence, trusting that it was all part of the same process of natural education—'that unto me the events/ Seemed nothing out of nature's certain course' (9.252-3). And because the Revolution goes so terribly wrong in Wordsworth's eyes, its catastrophe reflects back upon the subject of his poem, the growth of a poet's mind, and temporarily discredits it. Books 11, 12 and the main drama of 13 have as their subject 'Imagination, How Impaired and Restored'.

> This history, my friend, hath chiefly told
> Of intellectual power from stage to stage
> Advancing hand in hand with love and joy,
> And of imagination teaching truth
> Until that natural graciousness of mind
> Gave way to over-pressure of the times
> And their disastrous issues.
>
> (11. 42–8)

The 'over-pressure of the times', however, has been to give a licence to imagination in the public sphere, not to repress it. Wordsworth writes that when he landed in France, 'Nature then was sovereign in my heart,/ And mighty forms seizing a youthful fancy/ Had given a charter to irregular hopes' (6.34-8). Imagination itself creates the 'over-pressure' through its sympathetic aspirations towards a nature larger than its existing self-definitions. Hence those frequent descriptions of Wordsworth's political radicalism which employ a rhetoric familiar from his evocations of poetic magnanimity.

It is implausible suddenly to pose an opposition between mind and nature, so that the imagination can dismiss its revolutionary sympathies and return to a more natural course. The embarrassment experienced in 'London', where imagination was also found to imbue what it was supposed to criticise, returns. Often the narrator would dearly like to preserve the opposition, as the battle imagery tacked on to the Alpine celebration of imagination implies. But the true description of revolutionary excess is of a complete reversion to nature, typical of the childhood Wordsworth has been extolling.

> Youth maintains, I knew,
> In all conditions of society
> Communion more direct and intimate
> With Nature, and the inner strength she has—
> And hence, ofttimes, no less with reason too—
> Than age, or manhood even. To Nature then,
> Power had reverted: habit, custom, law,
> Had left an interregnum's open space
> For her to stir about in, uncontrolled.
>
> (10.604–12)

Nature rushed in to fill the institutional vacuum left by 'habit, custom, law'; and harsh words are said about the 'disgrace' into which 'ancient institutions' had been brought by their supporters (849–59). Their shortcomings cut them off from the true source of power which, as a result, lacks all control. But the tragic fact remains that the resulting direct, immediate intimacy with nature has been the tutelary spirit of the poem. Thus, remembering 'the glad time when first I traversed France,/ A youthful pilgrim', and in particular Robespierre's town, Arras, decked out in the trimmings of liberty, the narrator reaches for a tragic touchstone: 'As Lear reproached the winds, I could almost/ Have quarrelled with that blameless spectacle' (449–50, 463–4).

Nevertheless, the poet insists that he is describing his youthful mistakes—'juvenile errors are my theme' (10.637). But his point seems to be less that the equation of poetic and political freedom is misguided, but that it has not been fully understood. Poetry has been seen to define the limits of personal identity by showing the dissolution which, for Wordsworth, ensues when, in imagination, we push beyond these limits—perhaps through love of another person, but equally through love of mankind. The indeterminacies released by poetic vision return us to ordinary sights appreciated now more sharply for the failure of the imagination to find a solid foothold elsewhere. Both the failure to transform the ordinary permanently, and the visionary effort to do so, are inalienable characteristics of Wordsworth's poetic response. Directed at the politics of the 1790s in France, this attitude gives him a means of exonerating his youthful sympathies because they are true to something at the time (just as the search for a 'visionary' solution was true to the 'dreariness' of the boy's 'ordinary sight') and also because part of this truth is that they cannot establish themselves as positive alternatives to inadequate institutions. In this way, the implication of poetic and revolutionary sympathies in each other ceases to be a political embarrassment and becomes an alibi.

This is not how the narrator experiences things at the time. He feels placed outside his society, temporarily a genuine revolutionary: the declaration of war between Britain and France in 1793 pushes him, like Rivers in *The Borderers*, into 'another region'.

> No shock
> Given to my moral nature had I known
> Down to that very moment—neither lapse
> Nor turn of sentiment—that might be named
> A revolution, save at this one time:
> All else was progress on the self-same path
> On which with a diversity of pace
> I had been travelling; this, a stride at once
> Into another region.
> (10.233-41)

However, this place of disaffection is not geographic—
otherwise it would simply be France—but poetic, like the
greatness Wordsworth allows to Rivers. Even at its most
abhorrent and senseless, the violence of the Terror unexpectedly breeds in Wordsworth 'a kind of sympathy with
power', a sympathy once more explained by its own
imaginative resourcefulness in producing aesthetic affinities
which steady perceptions, as the child's are steadied when he
looks at the drowned man—'Wild blasts of music thus did
find their way/ Into the midst of terrible events,/ So that
worst tempests might be listened to' (10.416, 419–21).

At the time, though, as Book 11 has it, 'utter loss of hope
itself/ And things to hope for' impair the progress of
imagination. The narrator's disillusionment appears total, as
he tries 'to cut off [his] heart/ From all the sources of her
former strength' (11.6–7, 77–8). The poetic understanding
appears contaminated, even superseded by events. Of poets
and historians we hear, 'Their sentence was, I thought,
pronounced—their rights/ Seemed mortal, and their empire
passed away' (94–5). The poetic enjoyment of nature has
become 'a secret happiness' (34), artificially distanced from
the public upheavals. What is to be done?

At first Wordsworth sounds a retreat—back to where
'Home at Grasmere' began, back to 'ordinary sights'. Nature,
it seems, never really inspired an interest in politics.

> ...Above all
> Did Nature bring again this wiser mood,
> More deeply reestablished in my soul,
> Which, seeing little worthy or sublime
> In what we blazon with the pompous names
> Of power and action, early tutored me
> To look with feelings of fraternal love
> Upon those unassuming things that hold
> A silent station in this beauteous world......

The promise of the present time retired
Into its true proportion; sanguine schemes,
Ambitious virtues, pleased me less; I sought
For good in the familiar face of life,
And built thereon my hopes of good to come.
                                   (12.47–52, 64–8)

However, those passages in Book 12 sound unconvincing just after the 'spots of time' descriptions, originally in the first part of the 1799 *Prelude*, but now concluding Book 11. Wordsworth begins this Book by seeming to dismiss the political crisis impairing imagination as merely a blunting of the perception of nature: 'how feeble have I been/ When thou wert in thy strength' (148–9). Again, that must represent the feeling at the time; but it is, after all, the spots of time and their perception of nature which initiate that process of self-understanding preparatory to the retrospectively richer appreciation by the mature poet of public events already recorded in the poem. The poem's revisionary 'time' is perpetually at work to revise the narrator's received or remembered standards of representation. What follows in Book 12, therefore, is not something 'unassuming' but an explicit résumé of the critique implicit in the earlier Books, with passing cuts at 'what we name/ The wealth of nations', the unfair division of labour, the misnomer 'education', the limitations of books and language, and ending with Wordsworth's desire to deploy in poetry 'A power like one of Nature's' as he sets out across Salisbury Plain on the journey he transformed into his first major poem.

All that is left for Wordsworth to write is a conclusion in which the narrator merges with his former self, and the maturity and self-knowledge required to write the poem are described. And here something goes wrong, which perhaps had to go wrong. The poem begins with the poet's inability to find a subject, and his consequent questioning of his sense of poetic vocation. It justifies the narrator's poethood by showing retrospectively the poetic logic governing his responses in childhood to nature, and later on to his society. The argument *is* a self-consciousness, progressively disclosed through the texture of his experience. In other words, it cannot be schematised or put in a formula, yet that is just what Wordsworth tries to do in his description of the ascent of Snowdon in the 'Conclusion' of Book 13. The moon, the sea of mist, the hundred hills, the breach in the clouds through which comes the sound of water—all are part of a spot of time which translates into 'The perfect image of a mighty mind' (13.69). This loses entirely the unfinished suggestiveness of the childhood spots of time, which generates a poetic sense of self by whose standards subsequent pretensions to perfection on the part of various images—educational, political, literary and the rest—were to be judged. This is still part of Wordsworth's 'Conclusion'. His meditation on the view from Snowdon returns to the imponderables of the poem, though aiming this time more obviously towards a religious goal. The 'higher minds' produced by a poetic education are those for whom

> ...the highest bliss
> That can be known is theirs—the consciousness
> Of whom they are, habitually infused
> Through every image, and through every thought,
> And all impressions; hence religion, faith,
> And endless occupation for the soul...
>   (13.108–12)

The meaning of the poem lies in the power of its descriptions to avoid being conclusive or definitive, in this way not failing but succeeding in their response to the world. The poetry cannot be detached from the richer consciousness it gives of things, from its critical force. The only proper conclusion to

The Prelude is therefore to read it again, thus finding 'endless occupation for the soul'.

Yet Wordsworth wants, impossibly, to finish his autobiography: he has 'other tasks'. Having established what poetic credentials are, he ought now to begin his great philosophical poem *The Recluse*. The trouble is that according to the argument of *The Prelude* there is nothing else to write about—only more of the same. The poem becomes a verse-letter in which Wordsworth tells Coleridge that

> ...now, O friend, this history is brought
> To its appointed close: the discipline
> And consummation of the poet's mind
> In every thing that stood most prominent
> Have faithfully been pictured.
> (13.269-74)

Wordsworth's failure to finish *The Recluse* is clearly related to this success. In the last few pages of *The Prelude* he see-saws between apologising for his poem's egotism, and claiming that its themes are universal. The final paragraph is the most confident. Wordsworth and Coleridge are to be 'united helpers forward of a day/ Of firmer trust'; and this millenium is to be achieved with 'the knowledge which we have', by giving others the poetic education described in *The Prelude*: 'what we have loved/ Others will love, and we may teach them how' (444-5). *The Prelude* ends by standing firmly on its own, and not, as Wordsworth has it in a letter, 'as a sort of portico to the Recluse'.

Chapter Six

New Resolutions

Poems in Two Volumes, published in 1807, is in the words of the Cornell editor, Jared Curtis, 'the poet's last independent collection of new short poems; starting with the 1815 *Poems* Wordsworth began the successive reprinting of all his poems under a unified yet infinitely expandable system of clauses'. This practice of ordering his short poems under various explanatory headings started with the 1807 collection which is divided into 'The Orchard Pathway', 'Poems composed during a tour chiefly on foot', 'Sonnets' ('Miscellaneous' and 'Dedicated to Liberty'), 'Poems written during a tour of Scotland', 'Moods of my own mind' and 'The Blind Highland Boy; with other Poems'. There is no strict connection between the titles, and in a cancelled Advertisement in the printer's manuscript Wordsworth describes the poems as:

chiefly composed to refresh my mind during the progress of a work of length and labour, in which I have for some time been engaged; and to furnish me with employment when I had not resolution to apply myself to that work, or hope that I should proceed with it successfully.

By now the reader should be alert to the advantages Wordsworth typically reaped from halts in his poetic 'progress'. *Poems in Two Volumes* is no exception. Both volumes are guarded, as it were, by an outstanding poem of vocational recovery ('Resolution and Independence' and the 'Ode', known from 1815 as 'Ode. Intimations of Immortality from Recollections of Early Childhood'), in which loss of purpose or vision is redescribed so as to provoke a new increase in imaginative confidence. But the collection is unusually varied, for Wordsworth, and also contains poems which thrive on a genuine relaxation of the poetic will to power, others which revive the Miltonic tradition of sonnets on public themes, and some which consider what happens to the authority of poetry once a 'new controul' of religious faith is given precedence.

The poems which are more successful in persuading the reader that their existence has significance independently of their attachment, as 'little cells, oratories, and sepulchral recesses', to the 'work of length and labour' do so in characteristic ways. Wordsworth's frequent use of reflexive imagery keeps the identity of things resistant to poetic sympathy. This can happen explicitly, as when the River Duddon is 'Attended but by thy own voice', the Green Linnet is 'Thyself thy own enjoyment'; or, it can happen more generally when the marginality of things along 'The Orchard Pathway' makes even Wordsworthian sympathy unlikely. Certainly, the domestic poems, as I argued in Chapter 1 was the case with 'Personal Talk', are always capable of opening up vistas larger than the public sphere in a manner analogous to the spots of time. In 'To the Daisy', the little flower teaches 'a wisdom fitted to the needs/ Of hearts at leisure', which suggests the knowledgeable idleness

127

for which such ambitious claims were made in *Lyrical Ballads*, and anticipates the Pedlar's 'eye of leisure' in *The Excursion*. But, for the most part, as the contemporary reviews of *Poems in Two Volumes* indignantly complained, the subjects chosen—robins, butterflies, daffodils, celandines, a sparrow's nest—are undeniably trivial. What the reviewers failed to appreciate was the art of disengagement which these poems displayed, the temporary purging of contemplation of its larger designs by one who had, in the words of the sonnet prefatory to 'Miscellaneous Sonnets', 'felt the weight of too much liberty'.

However, many of the sonnets are full of 'liberty' and usually in praise of it. Wordsworth provides another figure of this step aside from a centralised poetic project in 'The Kitten and the Falling Leaves', where the narrator is 'Pleas'd by any random toy,/ By a Kitten's busy joy'. The short, four-beat couplets attempt to lighten poetic observation of the obligation it exhibits elsewhere in Wordsworth's writings to render the 'motion and the spirit' of natural process: 'Spite of care, and spite of grief,/ To gambol with Life's falling Leaf'. Similarly, two sonnets on ships ('Where lies the Land to which yon Ship must go' and 'With Ships the sea was sprinkled far and near') toy with their subject's tradition as emblems of direction and purpose. 'What boots the enquiry?', asks the first; and the second notes that 'This ship was nought to me, nor I to her,/ Yet I pursued her with a Lover's look'. Such relaxed affection for the inconclusive comings and goings of things momentarily quietens the strong educational drive usually fuelled by any indeterminacy in Wordsworth's poetry, although it can suddenly intrude with equally uncharacteristic crudity in poems such as 'Gipsies': 'The silent Heavens have goings on;/ The stars have tasks—but these have none.'

The most famous of the 'Poems written during a tour of Scotland' are also less rehearsals of the exemplary life-style of the peripatetic Wanderer in *The Excursion*, with its exorbitant sympathies, and more the enjoyment of openly speculative parallels set up by chance encounters. In 'To a Highland Girl' we hear that 'I feel this place was made for her/ To give new pleasure like the past'. There is no pressure, as there might have been in *Lyrical Ballads*, for the narrative voice and the voice of the subject described either to compete or to merge sympathetically. The girl is not incorporated in some Wordsworthian 'household of man', but her local pleasures are innocently set beside the poet's in writing a poem about her to gain 'new pleasure like the past'. 'To a Highland Girl' was recollected in tranquillity probably at least a month and a half after the relevant incident recorded in Dorothy's journal of the Scottish tour; 'Stepping Westward' and 'The Solitary Reaper' appear about two years later. The mode of comparison the poet chooses, therefore, claims a feeling for the Highland Girl's experience in a way which will explicitly distance his own. Any closer kinship is carefully relegated to the hypothetical 'and I would have/ Some claim upon thee', or to the openly fanciful 'Thy elder Brother I would be,/ Thy Father, any thing to thee!' She remains 'scatter'd like a random seed', random in his experience because rooted in hers.

'Stepping Westward' also takes up the idea of the random evoked in an accidental meeting. The narrator, asked if he is 'stepping westward', answers

> ...'Yea'
> —'Twould be a wildish destiny,
> If we, who thus together roam
> In a strange Land, and far from home,
> Were in this place the guests of Chance...

Presumably he is travelling west and wants it known that he is doing so deliberately. But his allusion to 'destiny' effectively broadens the significance of what he was asked.

129

However, the more this journey west suggests an archetypal allegory of mortality, the less does it appear to be something he has chosen. The licence for expanding in this way on the particular sense of the narrator's reply is given by his own extended response to the glowing sky above him as well as to the original question.

> And stepping westward seemed to be
> A kind of *heavenly* destiny;
> I liked the greeting; 'twas a sound
> Of something without place or bound;
> And seemed to give me spiritual right
> To travel through that region bright.

Taking it as a welcome, a 'greeting', also lifts the question out of its particular circumstances: it only remains addressed to the right person by becoming universal, common like the sky. The last stanza continues the dissipation of the meaning of the original words into another order of significance as the acoustics take over.

> The voice was soft, and she who spake
> Was walking by her native Lake:
> The salutation had to me
> The very sound of courtesy:
> Its power was felt; and while my eye
> Was fixed upon the glowing sky,
> The echo of the voice enwrought
> A human sweetness with the thought
> Of travelling through the world that lay
> Before me in my endless way

The 'voice', 'sound' and 'echo' set in motion a potentially 'endless' series of reverberations. These enact the simultaneous displacement by a '*heavenly* destiny' of the specific sky, the passing sunset suggestive of it. The poem, then, looks optimistic, shrugging off an impending funereal or elegiac interpretation, the allegory of mortality, by means of its own metaphoric mobility. The challenge has to come from someone 'native' in order to raise the sense of strangeness in her words, stimulating the narrator to his 'enwrought' similitudes. In 'The Solitary Reaper' (as in 'To a Highland Girl') the language listened to is Gaelic, and the uncomprehending narrator is immediately forced into undisguised speculation. Again, there is a marked disparity between what he thinks the 'matter' of the girl's song might be and his own more exotic responses to the 'music' ('Nightingale ... Among Arabian Sands'; 'Cuckoo-bird ... Among the farthest Hebrides'). Denied the possibility of any sympathetic designs on the reaper, the poet leaves her to her work and openly gets on with his: 'The music in my heart I bore,/ Long after it was heard no more'.

I have space here for only a very limited discussion of 'Resolution and Independence' and the 'Immortality Ode'. Begun as 'The Leech Gatherer' in 1802, 'Resolution and Independence' seems to display the familiar pattern of a narrator's encounter with a character and scene whose banal ordinariness baffles his imagination to considerable poetic effect. The narrator thus allegorically resolves his creative and personal crisis: his idleness and despair, precisely because they are true to the dangers of the poetic life ('We poets in our youth begin in gladness;/ But thereof comes in the end despondency and madness'), are productive of poetry. If *The Prelude* can be constructed out of anxieties as to whether or not it can be written, 'Resolution and Independence' can turn the professional worries of the poet into the worries which mark out the professional. This costly rescue, which might otherwise appear to be of slight consolation, is made bearable by the figure of the Leech Gatherer who reproduces, in an even more precarious mode of existence, the same uncertainties. The kinship avoided in the poems from the Scottish tour is built into 'Resolution and Independence'. The poet approaches the old man through a tripartite simile of 'Stone', 'Sea-beast' and 'Cloud'. The old man replies, courteously like the woman in 'Stepping Westward', also repeating *his* speech three times. Just like the poet, he appears to be motionless, detached from his environment in bookish contemplation, but nevertheless turns out to have been working, busy about his profession of gathering leeches. The narrating poet looked to him for a symbol incarnating reassuring messages 'from some far region sent', but actually hears his own medium and linguistic expertise reflected back to him 'With something of a lofty utterance drest;/ Choice word, and measured phrase; above the reach/ Of ordinary men; a stately speech!' Significantly, Wordsworth cut out five stanzas of the old man's speech from the first manuscript version, so foregrounding the appreciation of his speech. What should have been a disappointment, as the old man persists in his earth-bound tale, incidentally renders back to the poet an image of exactly the resolution and independence of which he needed reminding. The claim, earlier in the poem, that 'By our own spirits are we deified', cannot be proved by the example of 'the playful Hare' which, in the second stanza, is glorified by a felicitous natural phenomenon.

> The Hare is running races in her mirth;
> And with her feet she from the plashy earth
> Raises a mist; which, glittering in the sun,
> Runs with her all the way, wherever she doth run.

Nor, as we have seen, is there available a supernatural transformation. All the poet is given is 'the same discourse renewed' by the Leech Gatherer, 'stately' to the end, until he gets the point. By then, the fiction has it, he has written his poem.

At the end of the second volume of 1807, the 'Immortality Ode' balances the professional self-justification of 'Resolution and Independence' with a more inward apology for the kind of poetic vision available to the narrator. The language, too, is strikingly different, as suggested by the Vergilian epigraph, *Paulo majora canamus* ('Let us sing of somewhat loftier things'). The approximation of ordinary speech in 'Resolution and Independence', which inspired a number of parodies, is abandoned for an unremittingly 'lofty utterance' whose formality and solemnity might be expected to signal unusual poetic control and authority. In fact, as is well known, the poem laments the passing of a time when the poet perceived things with a visionary and dream-like vividness which would have translated directly into poetry. This apparently disabling incongruity between form and content is just what the poem tries to redeem throughout. The intimations of immortality which the adult can recollect emphasise what the child could not have realised: that, as shown in the spots of time, the vividness of nature was due to its having appeared to him as the sign for something else. The 'Ode' pushes this theory to its limits. Nature is so striking to the child because she has the novelty of a foster-parent; and the pleasure she bestows on him, 'Of splendour in the grass, of glory in the flower', are to make him forget more original glories.

> The homely Nurse doth all she can
> To make her Foster-child, her Inmate Man,
> Forget the glories he hath known,
> And that imperial palace whence he came.

That is why 'Heaven lies about us in our infancy', not because we are in Heaven, but because nature is busy compensating for it. It takes maturity, 'the years that bring the philosophic mind', to understand that all joy is founded on the desire for something absent in a world which, by

133

trying to recompense us for the loss, gives us not an image or representation but a surrogate experience for what is lost. For the child, all experience is vicarious, 'As if his whole vocation/ Were endless imitation'. Equally, the 'Ode's formal success in mourning its own loss of content to 'speak of something that is gone' is the only success we have a right to expect.

This is the heroic interpretation invited by a poem which cannot escape from its own crisis. Reading the poem in this way implies an idea of poetry as perpetually self-righting, as suffering no diminution from which it cannot once more profit and attest its own resolution and independence. The 'Ode' was written in two main stages. The first, probably comprising stanzas I–IV, was completed in 1802. It ends with a coda which, despite earlier claims that 'timely utterance' has given 'relief', returns to the dilemma from which it set out—'Whither is fled the visionary gleam?/ Where is it now, the glory and the dream?' The rest of the poem, dating from 1804, stages a second salvage operation of the kind just described, but at a cost of deepening the critique of present consciousness until there appears to be no defence left: there is an open admission of inferiority in what can be recovered.

> The thought of our past years in me doth breed
> Perpetual benedictions: not indeed
> For that which is most worthy to be blest;
> Delight and liberty, the simple creed
> Of Childhood, whether fluttering or at rest,
> With new-born hope for ever in his breast:—
>   Not for these I raise
>   The song of thanks and praise;
>   But for those obstinate questionings
>   Of sense and outward things,
>   Fallings from us, vanishings;

> Blank misgivings of a Creature
> Moving about in worlds not realized...

This impoverished existence, for which thanks is given, is then redescribed immediately in positive terms as 'High instincts' illuminating 'all our seeing', and culminating in the 'sight of that immortal sea/ Which brought us hither'. But the reader cannot help feeling that irreparable damage has now been done to the poem's argument if the penury of adult consciousness can replicate so effectively splendours of the irrecoverable childhood. On the other hand, a poetry incapable of being harmed by such admissions of loss begins to look as though it lacks any discrimination or authority at all. It stands in need of 'a new controul'; and the poem finally begins to gaze forwards, not backwards, in an unmistakeably religious direction to 'the faith that looks through death'.

This is the road taken by *The Excursion*, the way prepared for it by 'Lines, Composed at Grasmere' and 'Elegiac Stanzas'. In the former ('Lines Composed At Grasmere, During A Walk, One Evening, After A Stormy Day, The Author Having Just Read In A Newspaper That The Dissolution Of Mr. Fox Was Hourly Expected'), its title as lengthy and precise as those of Turner's paintings, 'Dissolution' is a surprising word to use to refer to death. It suggests the parliamentary disbandment of the good old cause of Whig radicalism, dying with its Francophile champion, Charles James Fox. Within the poem's imagery, Fox 'must die' like a Christ figure ('For He must die who is their Stay,/ Their Glory disappear') to be replaced by 'The Comforter'—the presence of the Holy Spirit which will compensate the disciples for Jesus's absence and for the lack of more practical divine intervention. But 'The Comforter' consoles the narrator before Fox's death, and clearly the poem does not translate Fox into the Trinity! Religious support rather replaces his inspiration. The Christ parallel implies that reforming political action may emulate ultimate values, but finally it must be resigned to the more modest realities of Christian doctrine. Fox's dying, therefore, sets in motion some of Wordsworth's most grandiose imagery ('this inland Depth/ In peace is roaring like the Sea'; 'A Power is passing from the earth/ To breathless Nature's dark abyss'), but not the figurative mobility with which his language used to track admonitions from another world. The poem, four-square like the great eighteenth-century hymns, formally accepts the limitations which are its theme.

'Elegiac Stanzas Suggested By A Picture of Peele Castle, In A Storm, Painted By Sir George Beaumont', is a poem in which Wordsworth allows a loss beyond all poetic recovery (the death of his brother John at sea in 1805) to press home its critique of poetic sensibility: 'A power is gone, which nothing can restore'. Two pictures are contrasted: the one the poet would have painted before his bereavement, and Beaumont's. The first is described in the categories of the vision desired in the 'Immortality Ode'.

> Ah! THEN, if mine had been the Painter's hand,
> To express what then I saw; and add the gleam,
> The light that never was, on sea or land,
> The consecration, and the Poet's dream...

Beaumont's painting is 'sublime', but this sublimity now contrasts with the privilege of poetic vision it has previously been associated with, and is valued now because it gives expression to common fears, terrors and what is needed to withstand them. The help offered is not an aesthetic, but a religious confidence, a 'hope'.

> But welcome fortitude, and patient chear,
> And frequent sights of what is to be borne!
> Such sights, or worse, as are before me here.—
> Not without hope we suffer and we mourn.

Of course, it all still makes for a fine poem; but the ulterior literariness here saves poetry not, as we have seen elsewhere, from its own ambitiousness, but from its modesty.

Epitaphs

'This will never do', began the review of *The Excursion* written by the Scottish critic, Francis Jeffrey. Especially unacceptable to him was a lowness of subject-matter, sanctified by religion. 'All sorts of commonplace notions and expressions are sanctified in his eyes, by the sublime ends for which they are employed.' Coleridge, on the other hand, writing in *Biographia Literaria* three years later, praised the religiosity of Wordsworth's poetry for showing 'the sympathy of a contemplator rather than a fellow-sufferer or co-mate, (spectator, haud particeps) but of a contemplator, from whose view no difference of rank conceals the sameness of the nature; no injuries of wind or weather, or toil, or even of ignorance, wholly disguise the human face divine.' The inactive, contemplative stance of the poet means that his sympathies for the characters are of no political moment. It is the very stuff of his religious faith to believe that their sufferings must be relieved not now but hereafter. In the same year as *The Excursion* was published—1814— Napoleon abdicated, and those who still implausibly connected revolutionary change with his imperial successes were reassured or disappointed. Wordsworth had also published in 1807 poems in praise of martial patriotism, such as the 'Character of the Happy Warrior' (1805–6) and the 'Ode to Duty', which describes moral obligation as 'victory and law'. His political credentials were not in doubt.

In the 'Ode to Duty' Wordsworth also regretted the freedoms which he had taken in pushing self-consciousness in his poetry—'being to myself a guide'—beyond the rule of conscience. By 1815 he had revised the fourth stanza to read:

> I, loving freedom, and untried;
> No sport of every random gust,
> Yet being to myself a guide,
> Too blindly have reposed my trust:
> Full oft, when in my heart was heard
> Thy timely mandate, I deferred
> The task, in smoother walks to stray;
> But thee I now would serve more strictly, if I may.

In fact, the 'smoother walks' were often those of duty, rather than the undiscovered country into which his imaginative sympathies and 'enwrought similitudes' might lead him. In tune with the 'Ode to Duty's' unadventurous moralism is 'Laodamia', published a year after *The Excursion*, in which the heroine is sternly and unfeelingly rebuked by the shade of her husband for losing her self-control enough to want to renew their love-making now, rather than to accept the religious logic of its postponement until 'Our blest re-union in the shades below'. Laodamia perishes 'as for a wilful crime'. She has not acquired the contemplative patience which *The Excursion* teaches. Emily, in 'The White Doe of Rylstone', written in 1807–8 but also published in 1815, has learned her lesson better. Her family, the Nortons, are destroyed in the Catholic uprising of 1569 against Elizabeth I. Emily is not only Protestant, but she also, as Wordsworth told Isabella Fenwick, 'knows that her duty is not to interfere with the current of events, either to forward or delay them'. She is a contemplator who finds in suffering a strange fulfilment. Discovering the death of her last brother,

> She reached the grave, and with her breast
> Upon the ground received the rest,—
> The consummation, the whole ruth
> And sorrow of this final truth!

The symbol of her unusual satisfaction in loss is the white doe which befriends her and answers the bereaved girl's need for love with a necessarily sisterly innocence, once more inactive and otherworldly in its implications.

> Her own thoughts loved she; and could bend
> A dear look to her lowly Friend;
> There stopped; her thirst was satisfied
> With what this innocent spring supplied.

After Emily's death, the doe continues to haunt the place where they were seen together. The doe is not a creation of Wordsworthian sympathy, with all the advances and retreats that has been seen to involve, but a substitute for real relationship. The purity of the love between Emily and the doe, emptied of immediate sensuous content, signifies the only values which will survive the fatal historical engagement of the Nortons. Emily is advised to

> ...be worthy of the grace
> Of God, and fill thy destin'd place:
> A Soul, by force of sorrows high,
> Uplifted to the purest sky
> Of undisturbed humanity.

The doe is there to grace this commitment to eternity with the trappings of temporary relationship. But the poem concludes by having the 'hoary pile', the ruined seat of the Nortons, awkwardly apostrophise the doe as being, by contrast, ahistorical and sacred, existing outside temporal kinship: '"Thou, thou art not a Child of Time,/ But daughter of the Eternal Prime".' And the metrical successes of the poem lie in its proleptic evocations of a ghostly, otherworldly presence which seems only incidentally to find itself finally in the shape of a doe.

> —When soft!—the dusky trees between,
> And down the path through the open green,
> Where is no living thing to be seen;
> And through yon gateway, where is found,
> Beneath the arch with ivy bound,
> Free entrance to the church-yard ground—
> Comes gliding in with lovely gleam,
> Comes gliding in serene and slow,
> Soft and silent as a dream,
> A solitary Doe!

In 'The Ruined Cottage', Wordsworth treated the contemplative stance of his narrator as a source of visionary sympathies frighteningly in excess of normal practical remedies. To turn away from Margaret was to return to the life of duty; a life in which 'I ought' implies 'I can'. In *The Excursion*, however, the long poem which grows out of 'The Ruined Cottage', the life of duty can eventually be equated with the contemplative stance because of its more obviously religious dimension. Forbearing from action, remaining as patient and resigned as Emily in the face of adversity, now expresses what has become for Wordsworth the deepest moral obligation of all—that of religious faith. The lowness to which Jeffrey objected in the main protagonist of *The Excursion*, the Pedlar-turned-Wanderer, expresses the egalitarianism only of a world to come: the common religious expectation on which the ultimate values in Wordsworth's poem are founded.

The Excursion established Wordsworth's reputation in many minds as the greatest living poet. Hazlitt's review of the poem, although containing almost as many strictures as Jeffrey's, also claimed that Wordsworth was 'decidedly at the head of the poets of the present day ... in a totally distinct class of excellence'. Shelley's first great poem of any length, 'Alastor', takes its bearings from *The Excursion*, and conducts an argument with a Wordsworthian narrator throughout.

For Keats, *The Excursion* was one of the 'three things to rejoice at in this Age'. Even Byron conceded that 'there is much natural talent spilt over '*The Excursion*'. All were suspicious of Wordsworth's peculiar 'system' of poetry, hinted at in the Preface, although the Wanderer inveighs against the man who, like Blake, would 'build systems of his own' (4.605). The lowness of characters chosen to utter philosophical sentiments is clearly still confusing, even when their religious orthodoxy is perceived. This is because the original narrative stance of 'The Ruined Cottage' is never quite effaced. Wordsworth's genius continues to be what Keats called 'explorative'. The title, *The Excursion*, suggests Wordsworth's usual awareness that he is still writing at a remove from the philosophical poem which is to be his life's work. At best, this excursion will be an 'intermediate part' of *The Recluse*. But *The Excursion* is also a parallel demonstration of 'the mind's *excursive* power' (4.1263), of the poem's own quality of figurative departure, of its successful failure to close on an essential meaning. It can thus either be interpreted as filled with a religious *contemptus mundi*, undetained by the things of this world; or else it still extols a frighteningly comprehensive sympathy which is never exhausted by any specific misery, possessing, in Keats' words again, the power of 'convincing ones nerves that the World is full of Misery and Heartbreak, Pain, Sickness and Oppression'.

The mind's excursive power is represented by the Wanderer; his faith is also invoked when a religious explanation supervenes. He is the main protagonist, or it is his life-style which the other main characters—Poet, Solitary and Parson—temporarily adopt, and his unfixed, travelling view of life which the poem follows. His companions find that they can 'with an eye of leisure, look on all/ That [they] beheld' (2.105). When the scenes they watch or hear about are tragic, this leisurely approach has the uncomfortable

141

passiveness of 'The Ruined Cottage'. The Wanderer 'could *afford* to suffer/ With those whom he saw suffer. Hence it came/ That in our best experience he was rich' (1.370–2). The Wanderer's mobility undermines the pretensions of any single life he encounters to stand for life as a whole. His 'happiness' in Book 1 challenges and shocks us. We move on with him from the ruined cottage, but worried and bemused that Margaret's story only ranks as an incident along the poem's way. His power to 'turn away' from her fate must be matched by the reader's confidence that the poem can have more to say. Wordsworth's initial, extravagant expense of suffering challenges us to '*afford*' still more suffering. One tale after another is emptied of its misery; and again, the only consolation seems to be that each narrative is not the whole story.

Often the reader is made to feel that *The Excursion* approximates to a series of epitaphs. Wordsworth wrote three *Essays Upon Epitaphs*. Essay I was published as a note to the first edition of *The Excursion*. In Essay II Wordsworth repeated his description of the graveyard in Book 6 of *The Excursion* as a kind of Eden:

> *one* Enclosure where the voice that speaks
> In envy or detraction is not heard;
> Which malice may not enter; where the traces
> Of evil inclinations are unknown;
> Where love and pity tenderly unite
> With resignation; and no jarring tone
> Intrudes, the peaceful concert to disturb
> Of amity and gratitude.
>
> (6.638–45)

The doe in 'The White Doe of Rylstone', it should be remembered, also 'Loves most what Emily loved most—/ The enclosure of this church-yard ground'. This seems a sad parody of the paradisial hopes of 'Home at Grasmere'; but, as in that poem, the meaning of paradise is unstable, sometimes indicating an intensity of perception, sometimes symbolising a world to come. In Essay I, Wordsworth writes that, 'without the consciousness of a principle of immortality in the human soul, Man could never have awakened in him the desire to live in the remembrance of his fellows'. The advice to the Pastor in *The Excursion* is to 'Epitomize the life; pronounce, you can,/ Authentic epitaphs on some of these' (5.650–1). But to pronounce an epitaph is to declare a beginning as well as an end, not only within Christian orthodoxy, but also with respect to the reading experience of the poem. At the end of each of the biographies which make up *The Excursion*, each authentic epitaph, there is once more the recovery of a beginning as the poem gets under way again.

In *The Excursion*, the ends of people often seem loaded with an inscrutable mortality. Of a day-old infant's epitaph, recording only its name and dates, Wordsworth writes in Essay III:

> more awful thoughts of rights conferred, of hopes awakened, of remembrances stealing away or vanishing were imparted to my mind by that Inscription there before my eyes than by any other that it has ever been my lot to meet upon a Tomb-stone.

In Book 2 the Wanderer describes how 'Oft on my way have I/ Stood still, though but a casual passenger,/ So much I felt the awfulness of life' (555–7). When readers hear an authentic epitaph in *The Excursion*, such as Margaret's, their position is equivalent to his: they stand still, before remembering that as casual passengers they can move on. The only way to be more committed and to carry sympathy further is to stop reading: to find a character's suffering so awful or important that they cannot bear any more or cannot accept its incidental status in the poem. That Wordsworth's success in evoking suffering might stop his readers is a faintly ridiculous notion. Nevertheless, if they keep going, the poem relegates them to the status of 'casual passenger' again, forcing them to acknowledge the practical limitations of their sympathies. Wordsworth's realism here is about as uncomfortable as it could be.

Unlike the spots of time in *The Prelude* or the argument of the 'Immortality Ode', *The Excursion* does not rely on the sheer vividness of perception to suggest an excess of significance whose meaning must lie elsewhere. As a result, its language lacks the complex self-sufficiency with which *The Prelude*'s opaque descriptive textures and unplumbed rhetoric drown any literal-minded reader who cannot bear the suspense. Instead, the poem is encrusted with Christian doctrine which grows more explicit in successive revisions. Book 6 begins with the 'Poet's Address to the State and Church of England'. He wants 'That basis laid, those principles of faith/ Announced, as a preparatory act' (6.88–9). The nation and its religion are the larger values which remain constant through each individual failure or tragedy retold in *The Excursion*. The argument works in the opposite direction to that of *The Prelude*: public institutions provide the standard for evaluating individual experiences, and not vice versa. But when political and theological credos are *not* explicitly appealed to as comforting certainties, the larger plot within which incidents are placed can seem to be nothing more than the provisional character of incident—the failure of each tragic narrative to become *the* authoritative pronouncement of the poem. This celebration of an inexhaustible sympathy, 'the mind's *excursive* power', is bound up with the critique of the character of the Solitary which is the central argument of the poem.

The Solitary is by choice reclusive and immobile, the poem's antithesis, living in retirement in his little valley: 'Urn-like it was in shape, deep as an urn' (2.333). His dwelling-place is an epitaph on his life, echoed in his pose later when musing in church: 'gracefully he stood,/ The semblance bearing of a sculptured form/ That leans upon a monumental urn/ In peace, from morn to night, from year to year' (5.214–7). The Solitary's peace is inert: 'Nor energy, nor fortitude—a calm/ Without vicissitude' (3.425–6); a tranquillity secured at the cost of any power of sympathetic response. Predictably, the Solitary enthused over the French Revolution, and his mind 'in a struggling and distempered world,/Saw a seductive image of herself' (3.804–5). He is a visionary on the Wordsworthian model, and his most striking vision is of 'a mighty city' produced by a trick of weather in the shapes of clouds and mountains:

> Oh, 'twas an unimaginable sight!
> Clouds, mist, streams, watery rocks and emerald turf,
> Clouds of all tincture, rocks and sapphire sky,
> Confused, commingled, mutually inflamed,
> Molten together, and composing thus,
> Each lost in each, that marvellous array
> Of temple, palace, citadel, and huge
> Fantastic pomp of structure without name,
> In fleecy folds voluminous, enwrapped.
>   (2.852–60)

In the next Book, the Solitary links this vision with the effect on his imagination of the fall of the Bastille:

>   From the wreck
> A golden palace rose, or seemed to rise,
> The appointed seat of equitable law
> And mild paternal sway. The potent shock
> I felt: the transformation I perceived,
> As marvellously seized as in that moment
> When, from the blind mist issuing, I beheld
> Glory—beyond all glory ever seen,

> Confusion infinite of heaven and earth,
> Dazzling the soul.
>
> (3.713–22)

But this visionary structure, unlike the first, tries to pose as reality. The 'golden palace' ominously recalls Milton's description of the hellish city of the rebellious devils, Pandemonium, in Book 1 of *Paradise Lost*, which also 'Rose like an exhalation'. The disappointment of the French Revolution is explicitly connected to an imaginative licence of interpretation which tries to find visionary satisfactions in political change. The Wanderer, expert in the logic of religious deferral, can explain such temptations:

> ...the innocent Sufferer often sees
> Too clearly; feels too vividly; and longs
> To realize the vision, with intense
> And over-constant yearning; —there—there lies
> The excess, by which the balance is destroyed.
>
> (4.174–8)

The Solitary's revolutionary sympathies had attempted to replace his hopeless longing for his dead family with something tangible, a new society. The Wanderer's advice is to recover a 'Hope' which, as it grows more visionary, grows also in religious, doctrinal exactitude.

> I, speaking now from such disorder free,
> Nor rapt, nor craving, but in settled peace,
> I cannot doubt that they whom you deplore [= mourn]
> Are glorified; or, if they sleep, shall wake
> From sleep, and dwell with God in endless love.
> Hope, below this, consists not with belief
> In mercy, carried infinite degrees
> Beyond the tenderness of human hearts...
>
> (4.186–93)

In this way, the Solitary's tendency to follow: 'the line of limitless desires' (185), as the Wanderer calls it, his visionary excursions 'Beyond the tenderness of human hearts', would have a theological sanction.

However, the Solitary's failures to 'realize the vision' force him into an introspective retreat at odds with the excursive temper of the poem, 'the mighty stream of tendency'. This stream is heard in Book 9 as 'A clear sonorous voice, inaudible/ To the vast multitude' (9.89–90) who otherwise, one feels, might understandably object to the Wanderer's solemn postponement of the alleviation of their sufferings until after their deaths. In Book 4, he had declared that even in the cases of political mismanagement and tyranny 'the law,/ By which mankind now suffers, is most just' (4.303–4), invariably deserved. Here is a political quietism complementing the religious resignation which argues that the insufficiencies of this world are salutary in fixing our attention on the next. Hazlitt could detect only an illusory movement in a 'stream of tendency' which left things entirely unchanged. 'The poem,' he wrote, 'stands *stock-still*. The reader makes no way from the first line to the last.'

Acceptance of the idea of theological redress for the wrongs of this world takes the socially critical element out of Wordsworth's imaginative sympathy. Christian belief also absolves his imagination of visionary presumption: the greatest height to which it can aspire is that of religious understanding, and there can be no harm in that. The importance of poetry as bearer of responsibility both for a criticism of institutional life and for ensuring that such criticism was politically innocuous has gone; and with it, the inner dynamic, the ebb and flow of sympathy, the slippings in and out of a visionary mode, the uncertainties of self-definition, the portentousness of ordinary things—all the qualities which provoked Wordsworth to ambitious poetic experiment. *The Excursion* is his own enormous epitaph, but followed this time by no new beginning. The poem's solutions and destinations prevent it from finally escaping the immobility of the Solitary it sets out to criticise, and make it impossible for Wordsworth's poetry any longer to celebrate as its own possession 'the mind's *excursive* power'.

Chronology

1770   William Wordsworth born at Cockermouth on 7 April.

1778   Death of his mother, Ann Wordsworth. His sister, Dorothy (b. 1771), sent to stay with relatives at Halifax. The following year he enters Hawkshead Grammar School, living in lodgings.

1783   Death of his father, John Wordsworth. Large debts owing from his father's employer, Sir James Lowther (Lord Lonsdale), left unpaid, causing financial difficulties.

1787   Reunion with Dorothy. William admitted to St John's College, Cambridge, where he is awarded a Foundation scholarship.

1790   Summer walking tour in France and the Swiss Alps with a College friend, Robert Jones.

1791–92 Revisits France in November, attending meetings at the National Assembly and frequenting the Jacobin and other revolutionary clubs in Paris and

Orleans. Befriends the Republican, Michel Beaupuy, and has an affair with Annette Vallon, the daughter of a Royalist family from Blois.

1792   Annette gives birth to their daughter, Anne Caroline, in December. Wordsworth returns to England a few days later. His guardians greatly disapprove of his intended marriage to the Catholic Annette.

1793   France declares war on Britain. *An Evening Walk* and *Descriptive Sketches* published, and *A Letter to the Bishop of Llandaff* written. Wordsworth walks alone through Salisbury Plain.

1795   After inheriting £900 from his friend Raisley Calvert, Wordsworth moves with Dorothy to Racedown in Dorset. Starts revising 'Salisbury Plain', begun the previous summer. During the next two years he meets Coleridge and Southey while working mainly on versions of 'Salisbury Plain', *The Borderers* and 'The Ruined Cottage'.

1798   Visits Germany with Dorothy and Coleridge in October, returning the following spring and settling with Dorothy at Dove Cottage, Grasmere, in December. Publication with Coleridge of *Lyrical Ballads*. Begins writing passages contributing to *The Prelude*, finished in its two-part form by the end of 1799.

1800   Starts writing 'Home at Grasmere', and continues composing new poems and a Preface for an enlarged edition of *Lyrical Ballads*, published that year.

1802   Begins the 'Immortality Ode' in March. Visits Annette and Caroline with Dorothy in August, during the Peace of Amiens. Marries Mary Hutchinson in October. The third edition of *Lyrical Ballads* published with a revised and extended Preface. Many of the sonnets to be published in 1807 written now.

1803 Settlement agreed with the Lonsdale estate on debts owing to the Wordsworths. Tour of Scotland with Dorothy and Coleridge.

1805 Death of brother, John (b. 1772), at sea. Wordsworth completes the thirteen-book *Prelude*.

1807 *Poems, in Two Volumes* published, drawing on work since 1802. 'The White Doe of Rylstone' written.

1809 *The Convention of Cintra* published.

1813 Wordsworth appointed Distributor of Stamps for Westmorland; moves house to Rydal Mount.

1814 *The Excursion* published.

1815 *Poems* published with a critical Preface: the first of many collected editions of poems old and new, frequently revised and reclassified, to appear over the next thirty-five years.

1842 Publication of *The Borderers* and a version of 'Salisbury Plain' in *Poems, Chiefly of Early and Late Years*.

1843 Wordsworth made Poet Laureate.

1850 Death of Wordsworth on 23 April. *The Prelude* published in fourteen books in July.

Bibliography

The editions used for reading Wordsworth's poems, criticism and letters have already been mentioned. The standard biography is still Mary Moorman's *William Wordsworth: A Biography. The Early Years* (Oxford, 1957); *The Later Years* (Oxford, 1965). Essential early critical responses to the poetry are Coleridge's remarks in *Biographia Literaria*, ed. W. J. Bate and J. Engell (Princeton and London, 1983), in his *Letters*, ed. E. L. Griggs (Oxford, 1956-71) and in his *Notebooks*, ed. K. Coburn (London, 1957-). Charles Lamb's fine review of *The Excursion* can be consulted, with his other critical opinions, in *Lamb as Critic*, ed. Roy Park (London, 1980). Hazlitt's essay in *The Spirit of the Age*, ed. E. D. Mackerness (London, 1969) must be read, as well as his related reviews and lectures in *The Complete Works of William Hazlitt*, ed. P. P. Howe (London, 1930-34). So should Blake's annotations to *The Excursion* and Wordsworth's *Poems* of 1815 in *Complete Works*, ed. G. Keynes (London, 1966). The variety of reactions to Wordsworth in contemporary literary reviews can be investigated in *The Romantics Reviewed, Contemporary Reviews of British Romantic Writers*, Part A, *The Lake Poets*, ed. Donald H. Reiman (New

152

York and London, 1972). John Hayden provides a guide to the subject in *The Romantic Reviewers 1802–24* (London, 1969).

The history of Wordsworth criticism continues to be a history of the main movements in critical theory from his time to ours. Matthew Arnold, Walter Pater, A. C. Bradley, F. R. Leavis and William Empson all made important statements of their own critical positions through their judgements on Wordsworth's poetry: see Arnold's Introduction to *Poems of Wordsworth* (London, 1879) and *Essays in Criticism*, 2nd series (London, 1888); 'Wordsworth', in Pater's *Appreciations* (London, 1889); Bradley's essay in *Oxford Lectures on Poetry* (London, 1909); Leavis's chapter on Wordsworth in *Revaluation* (London, 1936); Empson's '"Sense" in *The Prelude*', in *The Structure of Complex Words* (London, 1951). A highly selective list of the most influential recent work would have to include the following: On the early poetry, see Paul D. Sheats, *The Making of Wordsworth's Poetry 1785–98* (Cambridge, Mass., 1973). Mary Jacobus, *Tradition and Experiment in Wordsworth's Lyrical Ballads 1798* (Oxford, 1976) and James Averill, *Wordsworth and the Poetry of Human Suffering* (Ithaca, 1980) make the transition to *Lyrical Ballads* and after. On the distinctive techniques of *Lyrical Ballads*, see Stephen Parrish, *The Art of Lyrical Ballads* (Ithaca, 1973), John E. Jordan, *Why the Lyrical Ballads?* (Berkeley, 1976), and, best of all, the many-sided readings in Heather Glen, *Vision and Disenchantment* (Cambridge, 1983).

On *The Prelude*, see H. Lindenberger, *On Wordsworth's Prelude* (Princeton, 1963) and C. Salvesen, *The Landscape of Memory* (London, 1965), which remain rewarding treatments of *The Prelude*'s phenomenology. R. J. Onorato, *The Character of the Poet: Wordsworth in The Prelude* (Princeton, 1971) contributes to the psychoanalytic debate on the autobiographical status of the poem, and Frank McConnell, *The Confessional Imagination: A Reading of Wordsworth's Prelude* (Baltimore, 1974) makes sense of what Lamb called 'a sort of liberal Quakerism' or 'Natural Methodism' about

The Prelude's self-revelations. M. H. Abrams, *Natural Supernaturalism* (New York, 1971) boldy links the ambitious schemes of the post-Kantian philosophers to the structure of *The Prelude*, while Jonathan Wordsworth refines further on the ramifications of Kantian dualism in *William Wordsworth: The Borders of Vision* (Oxford, 1982). Difficult but definitive short studies have come from Neil Hertz on the 'blind beggar' in 'Blockage in the Literature of the Sublime', *Psychoanalysis and the Question of the Text*, ed. G. Hartman (Baltimore and London, 1978), which condenses ideas of the important Romantic critic, Thomas Weiskel; and from Cynthia Chase's exposition of the thought of Paul de Man by finding an allegory of reading in the 'drowned man' episode in 'The Accidents of Disfiguration: Limits to Literal and Rhetorical Reading in Book 5 of *The Prelude*', *Studies in Romanticism*, 18 (Winter 1979).

Jared Curits, *Wordsworth's Experiments with Tradition: The Lyric Poems of 1802* (Ithaca, 1971) provides a useful approach to the 1807 volume; and J. S. Lyon, *The Excursion: a study* (New Haven, 1950), D. D. Devlin, *Wordsworth and the Poetry of Epitaphs* (London, 1980), and K. R. Johnston's impressive rescue of Wordsworth's missing masterpiece in *Wordsworth and 'The Recluse'* (New Haven and London, 1984) do the same for, among other things, *The Excursion*.

John Jones, *The Egotistical Sublime* (London, 1954) and G. Hartman, *Wordsworth's Poetry 1787–1814* (New Haven and London, 1964) are outstandingly original and influential books; as is Harold Bloom, *The Visionary Company* (London 1962), which has a chapter on Wordsworth. John Beer's two books on Wordsworth, *Wordsworth and the Human Heart* (London, 1978) and *Wordsworth in Time* (London and Boston, 1979) are full of ideas. Francis Ferguson, *Wordsworth: Language as Counter-Spirit* (New Haven, 1977), Isobel Armstrong, *Language as Living Form in Nineteenth-Century Poetry* (Brighton, 1982) and J. P. Ward. *Wordsworth's Language of Men* (Brighton, 1984) contain particularly persuasive responses to the complexities of Wordsworth's rhetoric. David Simpson, *Wordsworth and the*

Figurings of the Real (London, 1982) explores, in addition, the relations between Wordsworth's metaphors and his politics, more flexibly and in more detail than I do here. Marilyn Butler, *Romantics, Rebels and Reactionaries* (Oxford, 1981) and Michael Friedman, *The Making of a Tory Humanist* (New York, 1979) illuminate further the cultural politics of the period.

The following collections of essays are helpful: *Bicentenary Wordsworth Studies*, ed. J. Wordsworth and B. Darlington (Ithaca, 1970); *New Perspectives on Coleridge and Wordsworth*, ed. G. Hartman (New York, 1972); *Wordsworth: a Collection of Critical Essays*, ed. M. H. Abrams (Englewood Cliffs, 1972); *William Wordsworth: a Critical Anthology*, ed. G. McMaster (Harmondsworth, 1972); *Lyrical Ballads: a Casebook*, ed. A. R. Jones and W. Tydeman (London, 1972).

In the Introduction I have quoted from H. T. Dickinson, *British Radicalism and the French Revolution 1789-1815* (Oxford, 1985), and in Chapter Two from Don Locke, *A Fantasy of Reason. The Life and Thought of William Godwin* (London, 1980).

Index